6 to **16** years

Child
Development

Tassoni

www.harcourt.co.uk

✓ Free online support
✓ Useful weblinks
24 hour online ordering

01865 888118

D0184075

Heinemann

From Harcourt

Heinemann is an imprint of Harcourt Education Limited, a company incorporated in England and Wales, having its registered office: Halley Court, Jordan Hill, Oxford OX2 8EJ. Registered company number: 3099304

www.harcourt.co.uk

Heinemann is the registered trademark of Harcourt Education Limited

Text © Penny Tassoni 2007

First published 2007

12 11 10 09 08 07
10 9 8 7 6 5 4 3 2 1

British Library Cataloguing in Publication Data is available from the British Library on request.

ISBN 978 0 435899 83 7

In-house team
Publisher: Beth Howard
Editor: Rachael Williams
Design: Georgia Bushell
Production: Jamie Copping
Picture Research: Chrissie Martin

Designed by Wooden Ark, Leeds
Typeset by Tek Art, Surrey
Original illustrations © Harcourt Education
Illustrated by Tek Art, Surrey
Cover design by Wooden Ark, Leeds
Cover photo/illustration © Photolibrary
Printed in the UK by Bath Press
Picture research by Liz Savery

Every effort has been made to contact copyright holders of material reproduced in this book. Any omissions will be rectified in subsequent printings if notice is given to the publishers.

Websites
There are links to relevant websites in this book. In order to ensure that the links are up-to-date, that the links work, and that the sites are not inadvertently linked to sites that could be considered offensive, we have made the links available on the Heinemann website at www.heinemann.co.uk/hotlinks. When you access the site, the express code is 983XP.

Contents

Acknowledgements

This book is dedicated to my own young adults Anne-Marie and Marie-Lise, who have proved to be a source of inspiration and support to me. Thank you.

Producing a book is a team project and this book has required the input from many sources. Firstly, in terms of research I would begin by thanking the children and young people who have kindly given me their thoughts and words, which I have tried to faithfully reproduce:

Anne-Marie Tassoni	Bekir Erylimaz	Ruth Bristow
Liss Zhua	Louisa Heseltine	Marie-Lise Tassoni
John Camp	Toby Gwynne	Molly Stones
Jake Faulkner	Louisa Gwynne	Stephanie Perfitt
Sophie Oliver	Harry Bristow	Victoria Perfitt
Nick King		

This type of book requires research and the collation of information. I must therefore credit and recommend *The Developing Child* by Helen Bee as being a good source of general information about development. I would also like to thank the organisations that have given us permission to reproduce materials and statistics. I must also thank Pebsham Primary School in Bexhill, as well as the parents who gave me permission to talk to their children. I would also like to thank Peter Dixon for allowing me to reproduce his thought-provoking and wonderful poem 'Booster Primary'. Finally, I would also like to thank the team at Heinemann who have, as usual, been extremely efficient and supportive: Beth Howard for guiding and moving the project on; Mary James for seeing its potential; Rachael Williams for her patience; and Ken Burns Brown for his copyediting. I must also thank Jennifer Enderby for her attention to detail when reviewing the first proofs.

The author and publisher would like to thank the following individuals and organisations for permission to reproduce copyright material: Peter Lindsay for the two extracts from the *Bexhill Observer*; NI Syndication for 'The things that wipe the smile off young boys' faces'; 'The sex lives of Scotland's children', copyright, the *Scotsman*; 'People in the UK among biggest users of cannabis', reprinted by kind permission of DrugScope; 'Pupils to face random drug tests at school', copyright, *Daily Mail*. Photos: page 1: Getty Images / PhotoDisc; page 4: Corbis / Hulton-Deutsch Collection; page 15: Alamy / Patrick Eden; page 21: Harcourt Ltd / Tudor Photography; page 24: Corbis; page 26: Rex Features, Harcourt Ltd / Tudor Photography, Corbis, Getty Images; page 27: Bubbles Photolibrary; page 29: Jupiter; page 31: Corbis; page 34: SuperStock / Image Source; page 36: Corbis / ROB & SAS; page 39: Getty Images; page 48: Alamy / OnRequest Images, Inc.; page 60: Alamy; page 64: Getty Images / PhotoDisc; page 68: Alamy / Ace Stock Limited; page 71: Getty Images /

PhotoDisc; page 72: Mark Boulton / CEC; page 74: Getty Images / PhotoDisc; page 75: Getty Images; page 79: Getty Images; page 84: Bubbles Photolibrary; page 94: Mark Boulton / CEC; page 102: SuperStock / PhotoAlto; page 103: Corbis / Eddie Keogh / Reuters; page 106: Harcourt Ltd / Jules Selmes; page 110: Masterfile / Rommel; page 114: Harcourt Ltd / Jules Selmes; page 116: Corbis / Larry Williams / zefa; page 123: Photo Researchers Inc.; page 130: Jupiter; page 134: Corbis; page 139: Alamy; page 145: Science Photo Library / Will & Deni McIntyre; page 151: Getty Images / PhotoDisc; page 153: Getty Images / PhotoDisc; page 156: Getty Images/Stone; page 162: Harcourt Ltd / Tudor Photography; page 165: Rex Features; page 170: Science Photo Library / Adam Gault; page 176: Rex Features; page 178: Alamy / Bubbles Photolibrary; page 180: Science Photo Library; page 183: Corbis / Peter Dench.

About the author

Penny Tassoni is a well-known author, education consultant and trainer. Her career with children and young people began as a teacher and she worked with children aged between 4–11 years in this period. Penny specialises in the whole spectrum of learning and play and is used for whole school inset training, as well as specialist early years training. Penny has also worked in a variety of roles for CACHE, the awarding body in child, education and playwork. She currently works as a reviser for their awards. Penny also contributes to CACHE's professional development and tutor days. She has written over 20 books including the popular *Planning Play and the Early Years*. In her spare time Penny is chair of A2P, a charity whose aim it is to provide resources that enable young people to find out about the realities of having a baby.

Introduction

Child development is a fascinating area of study. Having a good understanding of development is hugely important when working with children and young people as it can help us to interpret their behaviour and support their needs. The importance of understanding development is increasingly being recognised and this is reflected in the new occupational standards for the sector. This book aims to give the underpinning knowledge for the 6–16 age range, not only for those who work with this age group in any of a variety of settings (e.g. schools, youth clubs, after-school clubs etc.), but also those who may work with younger children too.

Structure of the book

The book is divided into five chapters.

1. An overview of childhood today
2. Emotional development
3. Social development
4. Cognitive development
5. Physical development

The first chapter looks at key elements of the social context of childhood. This is important as social context can impact hugely on development. The book then goes on to consider each of the key areas of development, starting with emotional development. Each area of development considers relevant theories and normative development, but often does so in the context of children's and young people's emotional well-being. This focus is deliberate as emotional well-being underpins development and this too is recognised by the new occupational standards. Development is also set in today's social context and the book explores many of the issues that affect children and young people.

Features of the book

This book incorporates several features that should make your learning more enjoyable and informative.

Interviews with children and young people Insights from children and young people of different ages to help you relate theory to practice.

Did you know? Interesting facts that provide a context about children and their families.

Issues Related issues in development that affect children, young people or their families.

Headlines Short articles from newspapers and other sources.

Observing theory Suggestions as to how you can 'see and hear' or test what you have read about. These observations may also be useful for showing your knowledge.

What does it mean in practice? Looking at how theory should relate directly to working with children in the 6–16 age range.

The story so far... A look at how previous development and early years practice influences children's later development. This feature often shows the benefits of good early years practice and its impact on children's later development.

Research it Suggestions for further research and study. These features may also be used for showing your knowledge.

Show your knowledge A series of questions at the end of each of the four development chapters. These questions might be useful if you need to demonstrate that you have knowledge of this topic.

I have enjoyed listening to children and young people and researching and writing this book. I hope that you enjoy it too and that it will help you with your studies or professional development. Good luck!

Penny Tassoni

A quick tour of development: 6 to 16 years

6–9 years

During this period most children are fairly confident and are likely to have strong friendships, although parents are still a major influence. Falling out and squabbles are fairly common, but children in this age range are usually quick to become friends again. Most children will have one particularly close friend with whom they often do things. Boys and girls are likely to play separately and have different play preferences.

For most children in school, classroom life and the playground are very influential. Most children will spend the majority of time with a single teacher and this person will have a major influence on them. This is a time when children have become aware of their achievements in relation to others. They also begin to notice the importance that adults place on them doing well. Speech is usually mature by 7 years of age and should be fluent for most children. Most children will have also learned the basics of reading, writing and carrying out simple number calculations. Whilst most children master reading and writing during this period, it can be very hard for those who need more time.

Physical growth in this period is steady and much slower than in the previous years of life. However, significant brain growth does mean that from around the age of 7 children's fine motor movements are far more skilled. This is reflected in the type of toys that are sold for this age range, which often have small and fiddly parts.

By the end of this period, children have usually mastered a number of practical skills such as dressing, simple cooking (such as making beans on toast) and tidying up. This is also a time when children begin to have activities and hobbies outside of school. Children may go swimming, play football, learn to play a musical instrument or go to organised groups such as Beavers or Brownies.

Key features of this age range

- Friendships based on play interests...page 74
- Separation of boys and girls when at play...page 76
- The development of reading and writing skills...page 142
- Greater physical coordination, especially of fine motor movements...page 157
- Increasing awareness of skills in relation to others...page 49
- An understanding of rules and their importance...pages 92–7

10–13 years

Friendships from this point onwards become central to most young people's happiness and emotional well-being. Friendships will help young people develop an identity that is separate from their family. A key feature of friendships from the age of about 11 years onwards is the number of friends that young people have. Friendships over the course of this period are often more stable with fewer arguments, but breakdowns are often characterised by hostility and are not so easy to resolve. Most young people will also be making a significant transition as they begin their secondary education. This may mean making new friends and also learning to find their way among a much larger cohort than when at primary school. Young people will also have to adapt to the new and larger physical environment, as well as the new experience of having several teachers during the course of a day.

A major feature of girls' development during these years is the onset of puberty. This can lead to a lowering of their self-esteem. Common anxieties include weight gain, breast development and overall appearance.

The amount of exercise that young people take also changes during this period, with girls showing a significant decrease in the amount of physical activity that they take part in. At the end of this period, many young people will begin to think about subjects they prefer and qualifications they wish to achieve.

Key features of this age range

- Strong and developing friendships based on characteristics...page 81
- Finding a peer group that shares their values...page 82
- Becoming more independent...page 67
- Development of more abstract reasoning...page 120
- Beginning of puberty for girls...page 159
- Changes to nutritional requirements...page 167–8

14–16 years

This can be a time when young people are under significant pressure. Conflict with parents is not unusual as young people increasingly strive for independence and development of their own identity. The transition from childhood to adulthood is not always an easy one. Young people may at times seem very mature, but still need and want to enjoy the last vestiges of their childhood, e.g. watching cartoons!

Friendships are still important and can be a source of support as they tend to be increasingly stable and are based upon shared values as well as interests. School life during this period can be a source of great pressure. Many young people are

A quick tour of development

usually working towards exams, although some may become disengaged from school and education during this time. This can also be a time when young people are drawn towards experimentation and so, statistically, there is an increase in the number of young people who begin to smoke, take drugs, drink alcohol and commit crimes. For most young people, such experimentation is temporary and is a way of creating an adult identity.

For girls, puberty, which began in the previous age range, draws towards an end at around 16 years of age. For boys, this is the time period in which their bodies begin to undergo significant physical changes, starting with growth spurts. Once started, puberty for boys takes around four years to complete. As with girls, this time can be a trigger for anxieties, especially if puberty and associated growth occurs later than it does for their peers.

Key features of this age range

- Exploration of identity through clothes, music and activities...page 47
- Move towards independence...page 42–3
- Exploration and development of moral codes...page 98
- Changes in body shape and appearance as a result of puberty...page 158
- Lower self-esteem...pages 58, 159–60
- Increased ability to reason and use abstract thinking...page 122

An overview of childhood today

The notion of childhood, as a distinct stage in life's journey, stems only from the mid-19th century, when it began to be reflected in social policy and legislation. Child employment was increasingly regulated, education to 11 years old was made compulsory (1870) and charities like Dr Barnados (1870) and the NSPCC (1889) improved the lives of destitute children. However, many issues facing Victorian society are still with us.

This chapter looks at how childhood is viewed today. It is divided into the following sections:

- Attitudes towards children and young people
- Children's rights and protection
- Education
- Poverty
- Crime
- Children as consumers

Attitudes towards children and young people

The United Kingdom has a reputation of being intolerant towards children and young people. Shops may, for example, display signs saying that no child under 14 is allowed in, whilst it is not uncommon for hotels and restaurants to ban children altogether!

The story so far...

Changing attitudes

In Victorian times, there were ambivalent attitudes towards children. Firstly, there were a number of sayings that are still well known, such as 'spare the rod, spoil the child' and 'children should be seen and not heard'. At the same time, children were seen as vulnerable and legislation was passed to protect their rights. Today, we still have this ambivalence towards children and young people and this can often be seen in media reporting where they are seen either as victims and heroes or, on the other hand, as pests and nuisances. Even in schools, children are not always viewed positively, as perhaps the title of a popular book on behaviour demonstrates: *How to get the buggers to behave*.

'*Adults always see you as a majority, rather than as an individual. They just make assumptions about you. If you were waiting for a bus and were going to let them on first, they would push to the front and assume you weren't going to. You don't even get a chance to show them what you are like. If you meet adults with your parents, they are totally different towards you. You are not a threat. It's as if the beast is tamed! If you met the same people on the street, they wouldn't make any effort to talk to you.*' (Nick, aged 17)

'*There are two sweet shops near our school. One won't let any pupils in; the other has a sign saying no more than three at a time. It's unfair. They wouldn't be able to have a sign saying "Only two Muslims" or "Only two Christians".*' (Mark, aged 16)

Boy banned from school because his hair's too short

A teacher at Bexhill High School told Richard Ellis, 12, on Monday that his close haircut was "unacceptable". Head teacher Mike Conn said the school rule was clear, that an "extreme" haircut was not allowed. Richard was informed he could return to school on Wednesday but would have to study on his own.

Young drug users find a perfect hideaway... in a church garden

A peaceful ornamental garden behind a church is being used as a cannabis inhaling den. Police have been alerted by concerned residents and are mounting a special campaign to counter the activities of drug-using youngsters who are vandalising the public garden.

Observing theory

How do the press view children and young people?

- Look at a copy of your local paper and a national paper. What type of press coverage are children and young people getting?
- Do you feel that this press coverage is a fair representation of children and young people that you personally know?

Children's rights and protection

One of the most important changes in children's and young people's lives has been the shift in attitudes towards them. Children and young people today are seen not only as having rights, but also able to contribute to decisions that affect them.

Chapter 1 An overview of childhood today

The story so far...

Development of children's rights and protection

In 1889 children were, for the first time in law, protected from abuse in a piece of legislation commonly known as 'The Children's Charter'. Until this time, children could be abused and assaulted by adults. In 1894 The Children's Charter was strengthened further with children being allowed to give evidence against adults and recognition of the notion of 'mental cruelty'. It also became illegal to deny a sick child medical attention. The Children Act 1908 also improved children's rights by establishing separate juvenile courts and also made it a criminal offence to mistreat or neglect children.

From these beginnings we now have comprehensive child protection procedures and the rights of children are enshrined in legislation (see pages 5–7).

▲ Children today have significantly more rights than these children did

Key legislation and initiatives

Legislation provides the framework for protecting children and also ensuring that their rights are observed.

The Human Rights Act 1998

The Human Rights Act 1998 came into force in October 2000 and has already had a huge impact on current legislation in this country. It requires courts and tribunals to make judgements using certain articles of the European Convention on Human Rights as a starting point. This act was not designed specifically to protect children but, under it, they are accorded the same rights as adults. This means that they have a right to dignity, respect and fairness in the way they are treated.

United Nations Convention on the Rights of the Child

In addition to The Human Rights Act, the UK is also a signatory to the United Nations Rights of the Child Convention (UNCRC). This was drawn up in 1989 and gives children and young people under the age of 18 their own special rights. There are five main strands to the Convention, which:

- reinforces the importance of fundamental human dignity
- highlights and defends the family's role in children's lives
- seeks respect for children
- endorses the principle of non-discrimination
- establishes clear obligations for member countries to ensure that their legal framework is in line with the provisions of the Convention.

The UNCRC is divided into articles. Table 1.1 shows some of the key articles that might affect practice with children and young people.

Table 1.1 Key UNCRC articles

Article	Provision
2	The right to be protected from all forms of discrimination.
3	The best interest of the child to be the primary consideration in all actions concerning children.
12	A child's rights to express his or her views freely. A child's view to be given due weight in keeping with the child's age or maturity.
13	A child's right to freedom of expression and exchange of information regardless of frontiers.
28	A child's right to education with a view to achieving this right progressively on the basis of equal opportunities.

Source: www.unicef.org.uk/tz/rights/index.asp

The Children Act 1989

As a result of adopting the UNCRC, new legislation was required. The Children Act 1989, which came into effect in 1991 in England and Wales and in 1996 in Northern Ireland, attempted to bring together various pieces of legislation. It is wide ranging and covers child protection and parental responsibility as well as the inspection of settings. The Children Act is especially well known for its stance that children's welfare is of paramount importance. It also made it clear that children's and young people's views had to be taken into consideration when decisions about their futures were being made.

(In Scotland, the UNCRC legislation was brought in under the Children (Scotland) Act 1995. This act gave children protection from discrimination, as well as ensuring that children's welfare was seen as of prime importance and their views listened to.)

The Children Act 2004 and Every Child Matters programme

Sadly, the death of 8-year-old Victoria Climbie in 2000 showed that there was still much more work to be done in terms of child protection. An enquiry, known as the Laming Enquiry, looked into the circumstances surrounding her death and its recommendations were taken up in a government green paper called 'Every Child Matters'.

This has now become a programme, which appears under various names but is generally known as the Every Child Matters programme (or just ECM). In 2004 a further Children Act was passed to implement this programme in England and Wales. The Children Act 2004 places a duty on local authorities to ensure that every child, whatever their background or circumstances, has the support they need to:

- be healthy
- stay safe
- enjoy and achieve through learning
- make a positive contribution to society
- achieve economic well-being.

The key implications of the Every Child Matters programme are:

- the creation of Children's Commissioners for England and Wales
- development of Children's Trusts by 2008 to bring together health, education and social services in a network
- an electronic filing system to ensure that, until the age of 18, information about children's and young people's attendance, health, etc. can be tracked

- development of statutory child protection teams called Local Safeguarding Children Boards, which replaced the non-statutory Area Child Protection Committees

- changes to training of adults working with children and young people, so that everyone has a 'Common Core of Skills and Knowledge'

- assessing individual children's needs through the Common Assessment Framework, a standardised assessment tool for local authorities to use

- an extended school programme (see also page 22).

It is important to know about Every Child Matters as it has enormous implications on the way in which everyone involved with children and young people should be working together. More details about the Every Child Matters programme can be found on the Government website 'Everychildmatters'. A link to this website has been made available at www.heinemann.co.uk/hotlinks. Enter the express code 983XP.

Involvement in decision-making

There has been increasing awareness of the importance of involving children and young people in decision-making. Schools, local authorities and various groups such as the Youth Council are starting to create forums for children and young people to be involved in projects and in actual decisions.

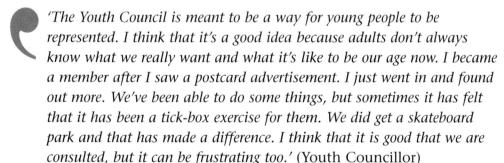

'The Youth Council is meant to be a way for young people to be represented. I think that it's a good idea because adults don't always know what we really want and what it's like to be our age now. I became a member after I saw a postcard advertisement. I just went in and found out more. We've been able to do some things, but sometimes it has felt that it has been a tick-box exercise for them. We did get a skateboard park and that has made a difference. I think that it is good that we are consulted, but it can be frustrating too.' (Youth Councillor)

In England, involving children in decision-making has even been embedded into legislation. Section 176 of the Education Act 2002 ensures that pupils are involved in some of the decision-making about issues that will affect them in schools. This means that most schools now have school council meetings where pupils and staff come together to talk about issues and plans, e.g. introduction or change in policy about a school uniform.

In April 2004, guidance called 'Working Together – Giving children and young people a say' was issued. The aim behind involving children and young people is to encourage them to feel more engaged in schools and also to help them develop skills in decision-making.

Protecting children and young people

We have seen that the principles of protecting children, and also giving them rights, have been established in law. However, this does not prevent abuse from occurring. In England in 2004 there were 15,200 children and young people, aged 5–16, on the Child Protection register, representing only those where abuse has been recognised. The extent of abuse will always be difficult to assess, but it is essential that everyone working with children and young people can recognise the signs of possible abuse and also understand the procedures for dealing with it in their local area.

Types of abuse

Abuse is usually grouped into four categories: neglect, physical, sexual and emotional, although some children and young people will experience multiple abuse. Some level of emotional abuse is involved in all types of ill-treatment, although it can occur alone.

Neglect

Neglect is the persistent failure to meet a child's or young person's basic physical and/or psychological needs. It is likely to result in the serious impairment of the child's health and development. It may involve a parent or carer failing to provide:

- adequate food, shelter and clothing
- protection from physical harm or danger
- access to appropriate medical care or treatment
- adequate responsiveness to a child's basic emotional needs.

Physical abuse

Physical abuse causes physical harm to a child or young person. It may involve hitting, shaking, throwing, poisoning, burning, scalding, drowning or suffocating.

Sexual abuse

Sexual abuse is forcing or enticing a child or young person to take part in sexual activities, whether or not that child is aware of what is happening. These activities may involve physical contact, including penetrative acts such as rape and buggery, and non-penetrative acts.

Sexual abuse also includes non-contact activities. For example, forcing children to watch or participate in the production of pornographic material, getting children to watch sexual activities, or encouraging children to behave in sexually inappropriate ways.

Emotional abuse

Emotional abuse is the persistent emotional ill-treatment of a child or young person such as to cause severe and persistent adverse effects on their emotional development. It may involve conveying to a child or young person that he or she is worthless, unloved or inadequate, or valued only in so far as they meet the needs of another person. It may feature developmentally inappropriate expectations being imposed upon them for their age. Emotional abuse may cause a child or young person frequently to feel frightened or in danger, or result in their exploitation or corruption.

> **Did you know?**
>
> A survey by the NSPCC in 2000 reported that eight per cent of the young adults surveyed said that they had never been praised at school. Eleven per cent said that they had never been made to feel special by adults.

Signs of abuse

Abuse can show up both physically (e.g. bodily injuries and bruises) and through patterns of behaviour.

Signs of neglect

Neglect causes children to be at risk of accidents and infections and can prevent them from learning. In severe cases, neglect can result in a child's death. Parents can sometimes neglect their children because they themselves have health problems or are not coping with their parenting role. Sometimes neglect is the result of ignorance, e.g. not understanding how to provide a safe environment or healthy diet.

It is important to recognise that some children and young people will be acting as carers at home. They may be carrying out most of the domestic tasks, such as preparing meals, cleaning and taking responsibility for other children. Some young people are also taking physical care of dependent adults. Table 1.2 gives examples of physical and behavioural indicators of neglect.

Table 1.2 **Signs of neglect**

Physical indicators of neglect	Behavioural indicators of neglect
Frequent accidental injuries (these are often the result of a lack of supervision or safety equipment)	Stealing food and drink
Being underweight and hungry	Taking significant responsibility for younger children
Being untidy and dirty, including their clothing	Reluctance to go home at the end of sessions
Being tired (this can be due to a lack of nutrition as well as inadequate sleeping arrangements)	Mentioning that they are often left alone
Frequent low-grade infections that go untreated, for example, nits, colds, influenza, coughs and earaches	

Signs of physical abuse

While most young children will have the odd bump or scrape, children who repeatedly have bruising and injuries may be suffering from physical abuse. In some cases, violence against a child can escalate and result in fatal injuries. Some children are given a cover story by their abuser to explain their injuries to others. The child might also be threatened with further violence if he or she does not use the story. The fear factor partly explains why children may not reveal that they are being harmed.

Children who have been physically abused are more likely to show aggressive behaviour towards other children, especially those who are younger. This is one way in which the child can feel empowered. Table 1.3 gives examples of physical and behavioural indicators of physical abuse.

Table 1.3 **Signs of physical abuse**

Physical indicators of physical abuse	Behavioural indicators of physical abuse
Unusually shaped bruises (these might reflect the shape of an object or fingers)	Aggression towards others
Bruises and marks on the body not associated with accidental injury, e.g. on the chest	Withdrawn and quiet
Burn and scald marks (including small burns from cigarettes)	Reluctance to be with a parent or a particular adult
Bite marks	
Fractures or swellings	
Cuts to the face	
Black eyes	
Difficulty in walking, stiffness	

Signs of sexual abuse

Sexual abuse in children is not always easy to detect because the child may not realise that the actions of the abuser are inappropriate. In addition, there may not be any outward physical signs because injuries can be internal or hidden by underwear. It can also be hard to detect because some abusers are extremely clever. They can gradually gain a child's trust (this is called 'grooming' and is now an offence) and, over a period of time, include increasingly sexual acts in their relationship with the child, for example, a kiss on the cheek becomes a kiss on the lips.

Sexual acts are also sometimes integrated with ordinary play and care activities, for example, bedtime and bathtime, or rough-and-tumble. Some children are told that activities are 'special' and 'secret'. Others may be threatened with violence if they tell another person, or told that something nasty will happen to a family member or person that they care for if they tell.

Young people may be more aware than smaller children that they are experiencing sexual abuse, but may not have the confidence or power to change the situation, especially if the abuse has been going on for a while. Table 1.4 gives examples of physical and behavioural indicators of sexual abuse.

Table 1.4 Signs of sexual abuse

Physical indicators of sexual abuse	Behavioural indicators of sexual abuse
Bruises, scratches and injuries that are not likely to be accidental, e.g. bruises to inner thighs	Regression in behaviour, for example, using comforters, rocking or thumb-sucking
Difficulty in walking and sitting	Inappropriate sexual behaviour, e.g. undressing other children, exposing themselves, sitting on the laps of people they do not know, trying to fondle adults
Fear of going to the toilet	Showing sexual behaviour in imaginative play, e.g. making dolls 'have sex' or putting a doll to bed and taking its clothes off afterwards
Complaints of pain when passing stools or urine	Knowledge of adult sexual behaviour, e.g. knowing the colour of semen
Genital or urinary tract infections	Unwillingness to be with a particular carer
Soiling or dirtying when the child has previously been clean and dry	Eating or sleeping problems
In more mature girls, pregnancy, vaginal discharge and sexually transmitted diseases	In young people, self-harm, promiscuity, running away, unwillingness to go home

Chapter 1 An overview of childhood today

Signs of emotional abuse

Emotional abuse accompanies other forms of abuse because all types of abuse result in children's emotional development and mental health being at risk. Emotional abuse alone can be hard to detect because there are no physical signs in young children. In older children, we may see self-harm, substance misuse or eating disorders. There are, however, various behavioural indicators of emotional abuse even in young children.

- Attention-seeking behaviours, e.g. a child is extremely clingy or deliberately provocative.

- The child is eager for affection and may seek it inappropriately, e.g. by approaching strangers.

- Telling lies to gain sympathy or attention.

- Regressive behaviour, e.g. baby talk or thumb-sucking.

- Tantrums beyond the age when most children have stopped having tantrums.

- Difficulty in socialising with peers.

- Tearfulness, lack of confidence and poor self-esteem.

- Self-harm in older children (see also page 61).

Children and young people who are 'hungry' for unconditional love and affection are very vulnerable. They may be targeted by paedophiles, who often recognise that the child's need for love may outweigh his or her reluctance to participate. Children and young people who are emotionally abused also lack confidence. This can mean that they are reluctant to try out new activities for fear of failure or humiliation.

What you should do if you suspect that a child or young person is being abused

If a child has a physical injury, it is good practice to ask the child how it happened. You should also mention it to the parent. You should be concerned if the child is reluctant to tell you how the injury occurred or if the parent is defensive. You should also be concerned if the child's and parent's versions of what happened are very different. Usually, children are quite keen to show off their 'war wounds' and tell you about them. In the same way, most parents will, on bringing a child to school, mention any injuries that their child has.

Sometimes children or young people will seek out the support of adults to prevent abuse from continuing. In other cases, they may unintentionally say something that is significant to us. The term 'disclosures' has been used to describe these types of events. However, this term is now used less frequently in court because the defendant's solicitors can then imply that adults have encouraged or led the child or young person to make a claim. The latest guidance from the Department of Health warns adults working with children to be aware that the way in which they respond to a child or young person, whom they suspect has been abused, can affect the later outcomes.

There are some simple but essential rules to follow if a child or young person tells you about abuse or says something that is of concern.

Do:

■ reassure the child or young person that you believe what they are saying

■ listen to the child or young person carefully, but do not ask questions as this may jeopardise a police investigation

■ tell the child or young person that you will do everything you can to protect them

■ tell the child or young person that you will need to talk to other adults in order to help them

■ reassure the child or young person that they are not in trouble and have acted properly

■ make notes in ink immediately after the conversation has finished and before talking to anyone else. Write down only what the child/ young person has told you. Do not speculate or add any comments. Include the date and time, and then sign the notes.

Do not:

■ promise the child or young person that you will be able to keep what they have said a secret (this is important because the child or young person can feel let down later and will not trust other adults)

■ question the child or young person or pass any comment other than to reassure them

■ make notes while you are with the child or young person or after you have discussed what has been said with another adult

■ add additional information into the notes later

■ talk to other people about what has occurred, other than the designated person for dealing with child or young person protection in that setting.

Where you should turn for help

Every setting should have a child protection policy with procedures for reporting alleged abuse and concerns. It is vital that you have read and understood these as they do vary. The focus of child protection today is a multi-agency approach. Police, social services and health professionals will be involved in making decisions as to what is the best course of action for the child or young person.

A useful guide to child protection has been published by the Department of Health, entitled 'Working Together to Safeguard Children'. It is part of the Every Child Matters programme (see page 6) and a link to this website, where you can obtain the document, has been made available at www.heinemann. co.uk/hotlinks. Enter the express code 983XP.

Outlined below are the groups that take the lead in child protection in England, Wales, Scotland and Northern Ireland.

Local Safeguarding Children Boards (England)

From April 2006 in England, Local Safeguarding Children Boards (LSCBs) have been coordinating local work to safeguard and promote the welfare of children. They are responsible for developing local policies and procedures for child protection. Boards include senior managers from all the key agencies that work with children and their families, including police and probation services.

Area Child Protection Committees (Wales)

In Wales, local authorities have formed Area Child Protection Committees (ACPCs) and are currently adopting new procedures. The document to look for, if you work in Wales, is the 'All Wales Child Protection Procedures'. You can download it by going to their website. A link has been made available at www. heinemann.co.uk/hotlinks. Enter the express code 983XP.

Child Protection Committees (Scotland)

In Scotland, local authorities have been directed to form Child Protection Committees. These have a similar role to the LSCBs in England. Further information can be found on the Scottish Executive website. A link to this site can be found at www.heinemann.co.uk/hotlinks. Enter the express code 983XP.

Safeguarding Boards (Northern Ireland)

In Northern Ireland, new proposals for child protection are currently being looked at.

Education

A major feature of most children's and young people's lives is education. Education became a right of all children in the 1870s when it was made compulsory. Over the years, there have been extensions to the original provision of education resulting in today's leaving age of 16. Schooling is free in all of the home countries (i.e. England, Wales, Scotland and Northern Ireland) although some parents will either opt not to send their children to school (see page 17) or may choose to send their offspring to private schools.

The start of compulsory education varies across the UK. In England, Wales and Scotland children have to be in education the term following their fifth birthday. In Northern Ireland the situation is slightly different. Children, with the exception of those born in July and August, begin when they are nearly 5 years old. In England, however, many children are offered places in school in the academic year in which they turn 5 years old.

In 1997, a Labour government was elected and declared that education was to be a main focus for their work. Raising standards of achievement for all groups of children, particularly those traditionally disadvantaged, has been the focus of recent work. The school leaving age at present is 16, although recently there has been some debate over raising it to 18.

▲ Most children start attending school when they are 5 years old

Structures of education

Each of the home countries has its own system and structure for education. The following sections provide a brief snapshot of the provision in each, looking at the period of compulsory education, which is usually 5–16 years of age.

England

In England, compulsory education is divided into three distinct stages: Key Stage 1, Key Stage 2 and Key Stage 3. In each of the key stages, schools must deliver the National Curriculum. There is great emphasis on the core subjects within the National Curriculum: maths, science and English. These are assessed at the end of each Key Stage using national materials and tests. Assessments are given great importance, as they are used for target setting for each school and also for the future performance of children and young people (see Chapter 4 Cognitive development). From 2008, a new statutory curriculum will be introduced for babies and children from 0–5 years. This will be named the Early Years Foundation Stage. In most areas, schools are divided into primary and secondary. Primary education is from 5–11 years and secondary education from 11–16 years. All schools are inspected by Ofsted.

Scotland

By contrast to education in England, the Scottish Executive leaves the content and style of delivery up to schools. Guidelines are given, but there are no statutory requirements such as the National Curriculum. Schools work with their local authority to determine the structure and content of the curriculum.

There is at present a 5–14 curriculum, which runs through until secondary schooling. This is followed by young people taking 'Standard Grades' in secondary schools between the ages of 15 and 16. Most young people will take seven or eight subjects, including English and maths. To provide more flexibility, the Scottish Executive is in the process of launching 'Excellence in the curriculum', which is a curriculum that will run from ages 3–18. The aim is that learning will become more personalised and young people will be able to take exams when they are ready, rather than according to the number of years spent in school.

Research it!

Look at the guidelines for primary schools given by the Scottish Executive about the amount of time that should be spent in the different subject areas:

- 20 per cent language
- 15 per cent mathematics
- 15 per cent environmental studies
- 15 per cent expressive arts
- 15 per cent religious and moral education
- 20 per cent flexible time to use on any of the main curriculum areas.

How does this compare to the National Curriculum in England? (A good place to find further information on the National Curriculum in England is the Department for Education and Skills website. A link has been made available at www.heinemann. co.uk/hotlinks – simply enter the express code 983XP.)

Wales

Wales became responsible for its education in 1999. This means that curriculum reform is still ongoing. Wales has a National Curriculum that, until recently, was not that dissimilar to England's. The curriculum is now the responsibility of the Curriculum and Assessment Authority for Wales.

A major reform has been the introduction of a Foundation Stage that runs from 3–7 years and also the move away from formal testing. Key Stages 2 and 3 run as in England and most young people in Wales will take GCSEs in Year 11. A major feature of Welsh education is the compulsory instruction in Welsh, either as a first or second language depending on the region.

Northern Ireland

Education in Northern Ireland is complex, as it had been devolved to the Northern Ireland Assembly which, owing to political developments, has been suspended. Reforms to the structure of the curriculum have, therefore, been postponed. The curriculum is the responsibility of the Northern Ireland Council for the Curriculum, Examinations and Assessment. There are four Key Stages in the education system:

- Key Stage 1 (4–8 years)
- Key Stage 2 (8–11 years)
- Key Stage 3 (11–14 years)
- Key Stage 4 (14–16 years)

There are assessments at the end of each Key Stage with, critically, children being tested at 11 years in order to gain entrance to grammar schools. Children take GCSEs at the end of Key Stage 4, as in England. Schools are inspected by the Department of Education's Education and Training Inspectorate (DEETI).

Home-educated children and young people

It is easy to overlook the fact that a growing number of children and young people do not go to school. They are home educated, usually by their parents and for a variety of reasons. Common reasons include dissatisfaction with provision of education in the area, bad experiences in school, or parents believing that they can provide their children with a more personalised system of learning.

Organisations that support home-educated children include Education Otherwise. You can find out more about this organisation by visiting their website, a link to which has been made available at www. heinemann.co.uk/hotlinks. Just enter the express code 983XP. Where children and young people do not attend school, their parents are required to show that they are providing a balanced education, although there is no requirement for them to follow the curriculum that is followed in schools.

School entry and leaving age in European Union and G8 Nations

Ages for starting and leaving school vary, though not by much, across all major nations. Details for European Union and G8 Nations are shown in Table 1.5.

Table 1.5 **School entry and leaving age in European Union and G8 Nations**

Country	School entry age	School leaving age	Country	School entry age	School leaving age
Austria	6	15	Japan	6	15
Belgium	6	18	Latvia	7	15
Canada	6	16	Lithuania	6	16
Cyprus	6	15	Luxembourg	6	15
Czech Republic	6	15	Malta	5	16
Denmark	7	16	Netherlands	5	16
Estonia	7	15	Poland	7	18
Finland	7	16	Portugal	6	15
France	6	16	Russia	6	15
Germany	6	15	Slovakia	6	15
Greece	6	15	Slovenia	6	15
Hungary	6	18	Spain	6	16
Ireland	4	15	Sweden	7	16
Italy	6	15	USA	6	18

Source: Economic and Social Research Council (ESRC)

Poverty

Defining poverty has always been controversial and difficult. However, what is not a matter of debate is its effects on the development and achievement of children and young people. This has meant that reducing poverty has been a focus for the current and many other governments over time.

The story so far...
Child poverty yesterday and today

In the 1850s there were many poor children. The type of poverty that children and their families were facing was 'absolute poverty'. Absolute poverty is the term used to describe circumstances where the level of income needed to support the basic needs for food, clothing and shelter is not available. In the 1850s this was often the case and poor families were reliant on charities and scanty state provision, such as workhouses.

Today, few people would argue that absolute poverty still exists in the UK, but children and their families do experience relative poverty. Relative poverty looks at the level of income required to sustain the generally accepted standard of living in a particular society. The Labour government elected in 1997 stated that it would bring an end to child poverty in the UK by 2020.

Did you know?

In Britain today, 21 per cent of children are poor (if poverty is measured before housing costs are taken into account).

The effects of living in poverty

Living in poverty has many significant effects on child development. In addition, poverty creates a cycle of social exclusion. Being poor can be an isolating experience, as it makes families feel that they are not part of mainstream society. This can lower young people's own expectations and aspirations for their future and can contribute to disengagement at school.

Statistics for children and young people who are raised in low-income families make grim reading. They are more likely to be involved in crime, excluded from school, have fewer qualifications and to be considerably less healthy.

Physical development

Children and young people from low-income homes tend to have a less healthy diet and this has associated consequences (see page 10). Reasons for poor diet include the availability and cost of food. Transport may not be available for families to take advantage of lower-cost supermarkets, or they may not have the funds to buy in larger, and thus more economical, quantities. Food is seen as a 'controllable expenditure', unlike rent. Thus, when money is tight, expenditure on food may be reduced.

As well as diet, low-income families may be living in low-cost housing that may not be in a good condition. Heating, like food, is seen as controllable and so there may be inadequate heating. The combination means that low-income families are more likely to suffer from respiratory diseases. Accident rates for children and young people are also significantly higher. This is attributed to poor amenities, lack of safety equipment and unsafe housing.

Cognitive and language development

Children and young people raised in poverty score significantly lower in cognitive tests. The reasons for this are complex, but families who are on low incomes are often unable to afford or travel to some of the enriching activities that other families take for granted, such as going to a library, music classes, swimming lessons or buying books and toys.

> **Did you know?**
>
> 'Cognitive' describes our ability to perceive, sense and understand things around us.

Cognitive development is also linked to parental interaction, but parents who are stressed and/or depressed find it harder to engage and interact with their children. Depression, mental illness and substance abuse are linked to living in poverty and interfere with this interaction.

Children and young people from low-income homes leave school with significantly lower levels of qualification. This affects their ability to find well-paid work and can perpetuate the poverty cycle.

Cognitive and language development are covered in more detail in Chapter 4 Cognitive development.

Emotional and social development

Being brought up in poverty can affect the emotional well-being of children. They may feel different and be embarrassed about their circumstances. Inviting friends back to their home may be difficult and so some children and young people miss out on being with others.

Emotional development of children and young people is partly linked to their parents' well-being. Adults in poverty tend to have lower self-esteem and more incidences of depression and this, in turn, can affect their ability to create an emotionally secure environment.

'I can remember eating and asking why my mum wasn't having anything. She said that there was not enough. When I was little, I also used to ask for things that other children had and was told that there wasn't enough money. I soon learnt that we were a poor family. I don't think that it is a problem growing up in a lone parent family, but it does make a difference being poor.' (Molly, aged 17)

▲ Where young people live in poverty they may find it harder to fulfil their potential

Initiatives to support children and young people from low-income households

The outcomes on development, and thus life chances, of children and young people from low-income households has meant that the government has been working to eradicate child poverty. The focus of much of the government's work to date has been channelled through a programme known as 'SureStart'. There are many facets to this programme, which include better education and health services for parents of babies and young children, and also more affordable childcare. The reason for providing childcare is to help families on a low income to gain employment. Unemployment is strongly associated with poverty and so the aim is to provide a route out of the poverty cycle by helping adults in families to find work. Tax credits, plus schemes such as the 'New Deal for Lone Parents', are supporting this initiative.

As well as childcare for babies and young children, the government is also encouraging schools in England to become 'Extended Schools'. This is linked to the Every Child Matters programme. The target is that, by 2010, all schools will provide services so that children and young people can be looked after from 8am to 8pm. This might be through childminders or through clubs, but the aim is again to help parents who need to work. Many schools are already providing breakfast clubs and after-school activity clubs. Some argue that this is helpful for parents, while others say that children and young people might be losing out by not being in group care for extended periods.

'My mum did go to work, but she could never do that many hours because of my younger brother. She always got really useless jobs as well that didn't pay well.' (Molly, aged 17)

Crime

The causes of juvenile crime and the strategies to tackle it are a huge source of debate, as undoubtedly it is a very complex area. Statistics on juvenile crime show that most of the victims of juvenile crime are other children and young people, although most adults may believe differently.

The story so far...

Juvenile crime

Juvenile crime was an issue that faced Victorian society and is still with us today. In Victorian times, crime was punished harshly, with children and young people being treated in similar ways to adults. This included deportation. In Victorian times, juvenile crime was linked to poverty and in some ways there is still a link, despite poverty now being relative rather than absolute. Family breakdown is also cited by some as having a significant impact.

Strategies for reducing juvenile crime

Successive governments have tried different tactics to reduce juvenile crime, which have ranged from 'short sharp shock' stays in juvenile accommodation through to the electronic tagging of young people. Currently, some juvenile crime is being tackled through anti-social behaviour orders (ASBOs), which were introduced in the 1998 Crime and Disorder Act. Their role was strengthened in the Anti-social Behaviour Act 2003 (2004 in Scotland). ASBOs are civil orders that, if broken, can be punished by prison. Alongside ASBOs, parenting orders have also been issued as, for some children and young people, difficulties in parenting have led to children and young people finding it hard to control their behaviour.

Youth Justice Boards

As a result of the 1998 Crime and Disorder Act, Youth Justice Boards were set up that work with Youth Justice Teams. The aim of their work is to prevent a young person from becoming a repeat offender. The team is multi-agency and is composed of someone from the police, probation, education and social services. This holistic approach has been seen as more effective than immediately using a custodial system, although England and Wales do use more custodial orders than anywhere else in Western Europe. The first stage is a referral order and a contract is drawn up with the young person. In the second phase some restorative justice is sought. This may mean the young person has to meet their victim or has to do something that directly links to their crime. If the contract is breached, the young person will then appear before a magistrate again.

> **Did you know?**
>
> In 1997, the age of criminal responsibility was lowered from 14 years to 10 years in England. In Italy it is 15 years, while in Scotland it is 8 years.

Is juvenile crime on the increase?

Whilst many adults worry about increasing crime, statistics do not necessarily bear this out. Each year MORI, the organisation that conducts many public surveys, carries out a survey that asks young people about crimes they have committed. These are known as 'self-reported' crimes. It is generally thought that this survey is more accurate than the number of crimes reported to the police, as many offences are likely to go unreported by victims. MORI's findings suggest that for the last six years the number of juvenile crimes committed has been fairly static. However, the cost of it has increased. In 1995 juvenile crime cost the government £1 billion; ten years later this had risen to £10 billion.

While most adults worry about juvenile crime, the victims are most likely to be young people themselves. Boys tend to commit more offences than girls, with the peak age of offending being between 14–15 years. Interestingly, the greatest predictors of whether a young person is going to be a habitual offender are the age at which they first begin and the severity of the offence.

Types of crime

Most juvenile crime is not serious, although it can be a significant nuisance. The MORI survey for 2004 suggested that the most common offences were fare dodging, hurting someone (no medical treatment required), graffiti and stealing from shops. Many young people who confess to committing a crime say that boredom, lack of facilities and places to meet are factors in their behaviour.

Research it!

Mobile phones are now owned by 95 per cent of children and young people under 14 years. Their popularity has, however, created an upsurge of theft and the 2000 British Crime Survey suggested that mobile phones were involved in 28 per cent of all robberies. The survey also showed that children in this age group were five times more likely to be the victim of such thefts than other age groups.

- Ask three children and young people whether they have a mobile phone.
- Ask them whether they have been directly involved in a mobile phone theft or have known someone who has.

▲ Many children now have their own mobile phones

Children as consumers

Children are now seen as consumers in their own right by many manufacturers and retailers, for products ranging from chocolate and confectionery to mobile phones.

The story so far...

Changing attitudes to children as consumers

Whilst toys were available for a few children in the 18th century, it was really in the 1880s and 1890s that children were first seen as consumers. Toy shops began to appear in large towns, with established names such as Hamleys being founded in London. Many toys were at first imported from Germany, including soft toys like the famous Steiff bears. This changed during the First World War when there was a ban on all imports from Germany. More British manufacturers were established, such as Chad Valley and Hornby.

The advent of cinema, and then television, after the Second World War increased the amount of direct advertising aimed at children. Today this is a source of controversy, as we will see later on in this section. The willingness of manufacturers to use advertising is not, perhaps, surprising given that toy sales alone in 2004 accounted for a staggering £2.1 billion, while the confectionery market is worth about £5.5 billion. A list of the most popular selling toys 1965–2004 is shown in Table 1.6.

Table 1.6 Popular toys – then and now

Year	Most popular toy	Year	Most popular toy
1965	James Bond Aston Martin die-cast car	1985	Transformers (Optimus Prime)
1966	Action Man	1986	Transformers (Optimus Prime)
1967	Spirograph	1987	Sylvanian Families
1968	Sindy	1988	Sylvanian Families
1969	Hot Wheels cars	1989	Sylvanian Families
1970	Sindy	1990	Teenage Mutant Turtles
1971	Katie Kopykat writing doll	1991	Nintendo Game Boy
1972	Plasticraft modelling kits	1992	WWF Wrestlers
1973	Mastermind board game	1993	Thunderbird's Tracey Island
1974	Lego family set	1994	Power Rangers
1975	Lego basic set	1995	POGS
1976	Peter Powell kites	1996	Barbie
1977	Playmobil Playpeople	1997	Teletubbies
1978	Combine Harvester (Britain's)	1998	Furby
1979	Legoland space kits	1999	Furby Babies
1980	Rubik's Cube	2000	Teksta
1981	Rubik's Cube	2001	Bionicles
1982	Star Wars toys	2002	Beyblades
1983	Star Wars toys	2003	Beyblades
1984	Masters of the Universe	2004	Robosapien

Source: British Toys and Hobbies Association

Chapter 1   An overview of childhood today

 Remember any of these?

Advertising aimed at children and young people

Currently there is a high level of spending on advertising aimed at children and young people, which over the past few years has raised considerable concern. The rise in childhood obesity has made advertising and children a hot topic. Currently, there is great pressure on manufacturers not only to change their products, but also to restrict how and when they advertise to children and young people. The term 'pester power' has been used in this context. The idea behind pester power is that children influence their parents' spending by encouraging them to buy products that they have seen on television and through the media. In 2005, for example, toy stores spent just over £7 million on advertising.

An interesting trend is the way in which characters from successful cartoons, television programmes and films are often used to promote both toys and food products. Looking back at the list of popular toys from 1965 onwards (see Table 1.6), it is easy to find several 'characters' that are used to promote everything from baked beans to stationery and clothes.

'I know that when I was younger, I wanted some things such as cheesey strings that were advertised on television. They always made things seem more fun. Now I don't think that I am influenced that much, but I do notice adverts in the cinema and often go to films that I have seen advertised.' (Lisa, aged 15)

Observing theory

Cut out three common brand logos whose products are often aimed at children and young people. Show them to three different ages of children and young people.

■ Are they able to correctly identify the brand logo?

■ Ask them how they know what the logo represents.

Research it!

Visit the Food Standards Agency website to find out more about food advertising and children. A link to this website has been made available at www.heinemann.co.uk/hotlinks. Enter the express code 983XP.

▲ Do you think that children and young people enjoy wearing brands?

Useful contacts

Bereavement

■ RD4U – a youth project organised by young people to support young people who have experienced a bereavement (www.rd4u.org.uk)

Bullying

■ Bullying Online (www.bullyingonline.org.uk)

■ Kidscape (www.kidscape.org.uk)

Child protection

■ NSPCC (National Society for the Prevention of Cruelty to Children (www.nspcc.org.uk)

■ Childline (www.childline.org.uk)

■ Teachernet (www.teachernet.gov.uk/childprotection)

Children's and young people's rights

- Children's Rights Alliance for England (www.crae.org.uk)
- Unicef (www.unicef.org.uk/youthvoice)

Drugs

- Frank – government website providing information about drugs (www.talktofrank.com)
- Drugscope (www.drugscope.org.uk)
- Cannabis Help (www.cannabishelp.org.uk)

Education

- Department for Education and Skills (www.dfes.gov.uk)
- Qualification and Curriculum Authority (www.qca.org.uk)

Health

- Department of Health (www.dh.gov.uk)
- Health Scotland (www.healthscotland.com)
- Mind, Body and Soul – government website aimed at young people (www.mindbodysoul.gov.uk)
- British Heart Foundation (www.bhf.org.uk)
- Eating Disorders Association (www.edauk.com)
- Wired for Health (www.wiredforhealth.gov.uk)

Mental health

- Young Minds (www.youngminds.org.uk)
- Mind (National Association for Mental Health) (www.mind.org.uk)
- Depression Alliance (www.depressionalliance.org.uk)

Social issues and research

- Joseph Rowntree Foundation (www.jrf.org.uk)
- National Statistics Online (www.statistics.gov.uk)
- Economic and Social Research Council (www.esrc.ac.uk)

Emotional development

The emotional development of children and young people aged 6–16 years has such a significant impact on all areas of their lives that this is the starting point for our tour of development. Emotional development affects the way in which they see themselves, the choices they make and crucially the way in which they interact and develop relationships with others.

This chapter is divided into the following sections:
- Personality
- Self-concept
- Attachment

Personality

A good starting point, when looking at emotional development, is personality. We are all unique and individual and what makes us so is our personality. But defining personality is quite a difficult thing to do. Is personality just about our social skills with others or is it about the way in which we approach problems or new situations? Parents who have more than one child will often tell you how different their children's personalities are or who in the family the child most resembles.

The Big Five

In order to be able to measure and study personality, some way of defining it is necessary for researchers. At present, the term 'Big Five' is being used by some researchers to look at five traits that seem together to define people's overall personalities and resulting behaviours (see Figure 2.1).

When these traits are measured, they are seen to be reasonably stable over time, although how effectively they can be used to measure children's personality is not yet clear. Some researchers believe that they can be used from middle childhood onwards and into the teenage years. For babies and younger children, researchers have been looking more at temperament (see page 32), but there is some thought that early temperament may also be linked to the traits suggested by the Big Five.

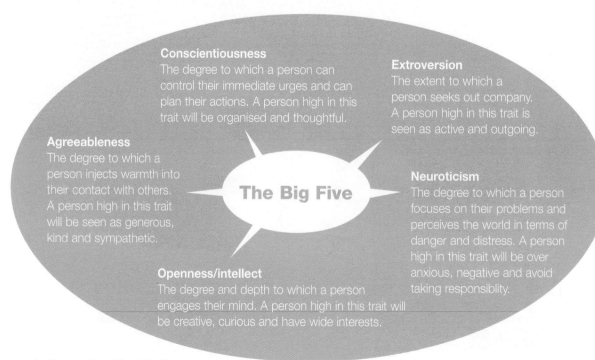

▲ Figure 2.1 The Big Five

Nature versus nurture

Where do we get the characteristics that make us the person we are? At the heart of many issues in child development is the nature versus nurture debate. This is particularly interesting when looking at personality, with most researchers agreeing that both are likely to be at work to some degree.

The study of twins

If personality traits are in some way genetic, one might expect that identical twins sharing the same genes would have identical personalities. Research does indeed show that twins have similar personalities, although correlations seem to be closer together in twins that are raised separately than for those brought up together. One explanation is that those brought up together consciously try to be 'individual' and so aim to find ways of not being similar. Thus, both nature and nurture are shown to be important.

▲ Are personalities influenced by our experiences or are we born with them?

The story so far...

Is a baby's temperament a template for later personality?

Whilst the Big Five (see page 30) seem to describe personality traits from late childhood onwards, work on temperament looks at the characteristics of babies and toddlers. By looking at babies from birth, researchers can see that already babies have different responses. Measurements of the frequency of crying, activity level and interest in others as well as how easily babies are soothed or become irritable have shown that babies' temperaments do vary greatly. Researchers Chess and Thomas (1984) have famously categorised babies into three types (see Figure 2.2).

Follow-up work found that the characteristics that babies showed early on continued into later childhood. However, it has also been found that some babies who were 'difficult' but who had parents who were able to respond positively and thus mitigate their behaviours were able to move into one of the other two temperament categories.

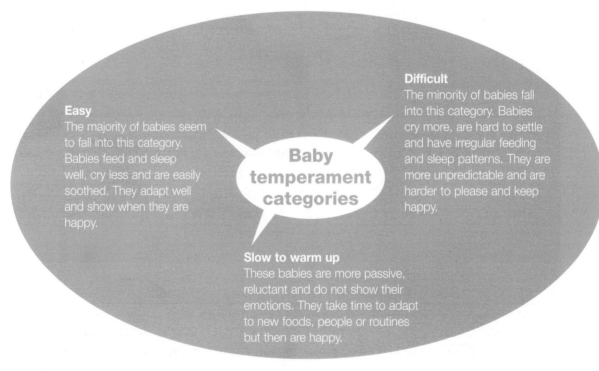

Easy
The majority of babies seem to fall into this category. Babies feed and sleep well, cry less and are easily soothed. They adapt well and show when they are happy.

Difficult
The minority of babies fall into this category. Babies cry more, are hard to settle and have irregular feeding and sleep patterns. They are more unpredictable and are harder to please and keep happy.

Baby temperament categories

Slow to warm up
These babies are more passive, reluctant and do not show their emotions. They take time to adapt to new foods, people or routines but then are happy.

▲ **Figure 2.2** Baby temperament categories

Extrovert or introvert – is this genetic?

In support of nature in the nature versus nurture debate, there are biological explanations that might account for differences in personality. Some children and young people are noticeably averse to change or new experiences. They may dislike crowds or meeting new people and this can show itself very early on. The biological approach suggests that this is down to levels of arousal, with some people easily aroused whilst others much less so. Geneticists have even found the gene that they believe may be partly responsible for this: D4DR.

Children who are easily aroused will find change or new experiences literally 'too much', as this provides them with an excessive amount of arousal. As the brain tries to regulate arousal levels they will find these experiences unpleasant. Conversely, children and young people whose levels of arousal are pegged lower will actively look for new experiences and ways of gaining stimulation.

Issues – Risk-taking behaviours

Children and young people who are under aroused are likely to be constantly looking for new experiences, sensations and stimuli. For some children and young people this may get them into trouble as they may find it hard to sit still and concentrate, for example, when in school. Practical lessons are therefore more popular for these children, as by physically moving, talking and being active, the body becomes more aroused. In extreme cases, it may also be one of the reasons why some young people try out drugs or other risk-taking activities.

Learning theory explanations of personality

We have seen that there might be some evidence that personality development is explained using a biological model. Learning explanations of personality focus on the way in which experiences might be involved in shaping aspects of personality, e.g. how parents react. With learning theories, experiences are seen as more important than biological input. Over the next few pages we will look at how parents and birth order might be influential in children's personality development, as well as two learning theories that might also explain how some aspects of behaviour might be learned or reinforced.

Parental influence

Parenting is a key influence on shaping personality, although it is far from being the only factor. This is well illustrated by the way in which siblings generally turn out differently, even though their parents' values and overall attitudes towards discipline are unlikely to change. But measuring parental influence is exceptionally difficult. Parents generally respond in different ways to each of their children, even though the differences may be quite subtle. Boys are often treated differently from girls, whilst older and younger children may have different experiences. As we saw with temperament, parents can moderate the outcomes depending on how they respond to their child. An anxious parent may make a shy child shyer. A more relaxed parent may send out calming signals to their child, which allows the child's fearfulness and thus levels of arousal to reduce. This means that, in theory, parents should try to adapt their parenting style to meet the needs of the child. What works with one child might not work with another. Many parents instinctively know this, but may not feel that it is fair to take a different approach.

Behaviourist approaches to personality

Whilst most researchers believe that personality is intertwined with some hereditary component, there is a school of thought that believes that babies, children and young people develop traits according to the way in which these are reinforced. Thus a child who shows shy behaviour and is given adult encouragement, attention or even criticism, gains reinforcement for its shyness, so is more likely to err towards shy behaviour in situations that are similar in the future.

It is also argued that the stability of some traits is linked to the way in which reinforcement is 'partially' reinforced. Partial reinforcement is where sometimes reinforcement is given and sometimes not. One day an adult may notice and react to the child's shy behaviour but another day may decide not to say anything. This on/off reinforcement schedule is rarely planned by the adults, but nevertheless is extremely powerful. Adults working or being with children and young people are invariably inconsistent! In experiments, partial reinforcement is shown to produce lasting behaviours.

▲ This parent recognises that this child needs reassurance

Aggression in children and young people is sometimes the result of an inconsistent approach from adults. Parents who sometimes allow their children to be quite aggressive but at other times physically punish them for being aggressive, are more likely to find that their children show persistent aggressive tendencies.

Social cognitive theory: learning through modelling and reinforcement

As well as reinforcement, some psychologists, the most influential of whom is Albert Bandura, suggest that another process is also taking place: modelling. Their argument is that children learn characteristics from watching and absorbing them from others, notably their parents and carers, but also peers and even media images. Thus a child who sees that their parents often help others is more likely to model this aspect, whilst a child who hears their parents moaning and being impatient in queues may again copy this.

Whilst parents and teachers are no doubt influential, long-term exposure to antisocial behaviour is also thought to have an effect. A young person growing up in an environment where others carry knives, swear and respond to situations with aggression may also become more aggressive. It is even argued that this type of environment may tip the balance away from the influence of parents.

Finally, Bandura also argues that it is not just the behaviours that children and young people are absorbing, but also the expectations, values and attitudes of those they are with. The child, through watching and also the reinforcement that is received, begins to develop its own set of assumptions or rules. These then become the benchmark that the child or young person uses to shape their responses.

Birth order and personality

Can your place within a family make a difference to your personality? Some research does indeed show that it might make a slight difference, although according to Bee (2006) it might be less a question of birth order, more about each child or young person trying to create an individual role in the family. The argument is that each child must find their own way or niche in a family structure.

First borns

There is some evidence to show that first borns in a family are more likely to 'toe the line', take on responsibility and be achievement-orientated. In later life they are also more likely to take established routes through their careers.

Bee suggests that this is linked to the way in which parents focus on the child and are learning how to parent. Parents are likely to have higher expectations and be more controlling and protective in their style.

Subsequent children

First born children have some advantages, as they may have cornered the market in terms of achievement and also parental attention. Subsequent children therefore may take different paths. They are more likely to be independent, creative and even rebellious.

▲ Can birth order make a difference to personality?

Exceptions

There are, of course, plenty of exceptions to the birth order stereotypes, so it is important that some degree of scepticism is retained. One explanation for differences is that sometimes the first born child does not take up the mantle of being the conformist, nor take on the responsibility or maturity roles that are usually expected. This means that another child within the family may develop this role instead. Gender too can play a part, as boys and girls are often treated differently within a family.

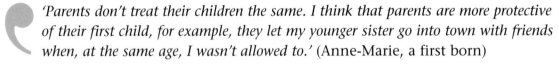

'Parents don't treat their children the same. I think that parents are more protective of their first child, for example, they let my younger sister go into town with friends when, at the same age, I wasn't allowed to.' (Anne-Marie, a first born)

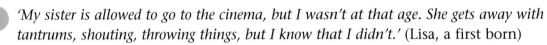

'My sister is allowed to go to the cinema, but I wasn't at that age. She gets away with tantrums, shouting, throwing things, but I know that I didn't.' (Lisa, a first born)

Gender, parents and personality

Most parents would accept that, if they have both boys and girls, they do interact with them differently, although interestingly not all realise that they may have different expectations and boundaries. A fascinating question, and one that is probably hard to resolve, is how does this affect personality?

Research suggests that parents comment on, and encourage even early on, the activity level of boys, as this is seen as typical behaviour for boys. For girls the converse is true, with staying still being favourably commented upon, and some parents even curbing exuberance as this is seen as aggressive.

Psychoanalytical theories of personality

The two key and most influential theories of psychoanalytical personality development are those of Freud and Erikson. They differ from others in that they suggest that personality is something that develops over time and is staged, with children's and young people's personality being determined as a consequence of how they fare in each stage. Both Freud's and Erikson's theories suggest that resulting personality will be linked to the relationship that a child has with key people in their lives, notably parents. In this respect, there is a link with the 'nurture' theories of personality.

Freud

One of the greatest influences in psychology is Sigmund Freud. He is particularly famous for his psychosexual theory of development, which is often used to explain our unconscious thoughts and actions. He was one of the first people to consider the ways in which our personalities were constructed. He suggested that there are three parts that make up our personality: the id, the ego and the superego. Not all are present at birth but develop with the child.

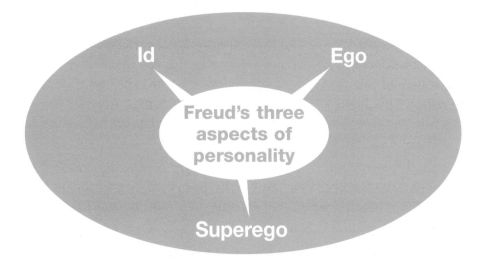

▲ **Figure 2.3** Freud's three aspects of personality

The id

This is the instinctive part of our personality. It is governed by the drives and needs of the body, such as hunger and finding pleasure. The id does not consider how meeting our desires and wants will affect others, so it is often thought of as the selfish and passionate component. Freud suggested that when babies are born they only have the id. Hence a baby will cry and cry until it gets fed, regardless of how tired the carer is or whether there are other children that also need feeding. Getting a desire or need met is known as 'gratification'.

The ego

The ego has a planning role. It works out how to meet the id's needs and desires in the best way. The ego develops from the id in the first few months; for example, babies might learn that by smiling in some situations they are more likely to get their needs met, whilst in others it is better to cry. In some situations the ego may make the id wait for its demands to be met. For example, a child may learn that if they snatch a cake from a tray they may have it taken away from them, but by waiting to be offered a cake they will eventually get it. The term 'deferred gratification' is used when this happens. The ego is often thought of as being the common-sense part of our personalities.

The superego

The superego develops later in childhood. It tries to control the id and ego and comprises two elements:

1.   the conscience

2.   the ego-ideal.

The conscience will punish the ego if it misbehaves, i.e. does something that the superego considers to be wrong, such as stealing the cake from the tray. This is the source of our guilt. The ego-ideal will reward the ego if it shows good behaviour. This is the source of our pride and confidence.

Conflict within our personalities

The ego is caught between the id and the superego. It needs to satisfy the id's strong demands, but does not want to be punished by the superego. This means that there is often conflict within ourselves and the ego has to try to find a solution.

You see a cake on a tray. You are hungry and you just want to take it and eat it. Your ego stops you from doing this because you might get into trouble. Your id is still not happy and you are very hungry. You then realise that no one else is around, so you will not get caught. This is tempting but the superego steps in.

▲ Young children find it hard to resist temptation! Maybe the id is at work

The conscience part of the superego threatens the ego with punishment, i.e. guilt. You decide not to take the cake but to find out if it is going spare.

Some conflicts are not so easy to resolve. Freud suggested that unresolved conflicts show themselves in three main ways.

1. **Dreams** Problems and conflicts are dreamt about as our unconscious minds are wrestling with them.

2. **Neurotic symptoms** We may develop physical symptoms as a result of conflict.

3. **Defence mechanisms** We may use a variety of strategies to try to forget that there is a conflict. These include repression, denial and projection.

Freud's psychosexual stages

Freud believed that our personalities are based mainly on biological needs or drives – the id factor. He felt that the main drives were sexual and aggressive and he shocked Victorian and Edwardian society by suggesting that the sexual drive was present in babies and children. Freud called the energy behind these drives 'libido'.

He suggested that there are five stages through which we pass in childhood and on which our libido is concentrated. The stages are linked to physical development of the body. Freud felt that if we do not pass through these stages satisfactorily, part of our energy or libido will be stuck or 'fixated'. This will affect our behaviour and personality (see Table 2.1).

Table 2.1 **Freud's five psychosexual stages**

Age	Stage	Developmental stage	Potential personality/behavioural traits if 'fixed' during stage
0–1	Oral	Weaning	Incredulous, naive – swallowing anything that someone says Behaviours involving the mouth, e.g. smoking, sucking pens, overeating
1–3	Anal	Toilet training	Personality traits, if trained before ready, include 'retentive' behaviours such as refusing to share, being mean-spirited as well as excessively tidy or compulsive Reverse traits for children who are left in nappies for too long include being overgenerous and loud
3–5	Phallic	Resolution of Oedipus complex (see below)	Vanity, impulsiveness, low sense of worth, over cautious
5–12	Latency	Development of ego defence mechanisms	None – this is a calmer period for children
12–18	Genital	Interest in sexual activity and intimacy	Dependent on previous stages, but should be sexually mature and ready for intimacy

Oedipus complex

One of the theories that made Freud famous is the Oedipus complex. In the Greek tragedy, a man named Oedipus kills his father and falls in love with his mother. Freud suggests that in the phallic stage, children fall in love with the opposite-sex parent, hence the title of the theory. They then see the other parent as a rival. This is also a stage where children become aware of the physical differences between men and women. Freud believed that the absence of a penis is thought by children to be as a result of castration. This leads boys to fear of being castrated: 'castration anxiety'. Boys, therefore, have a decision to make: should they continue to love their mothers and risk being castrated by their fathers? Freud suggests that the conflict is resolved because boys decide to try to make a friend of their fathers by copying and admiring them.

For girls the situation is slightly different. Girls will believe that they have already been castrated and so develop 'penis envy'. Eventually realising that they cannot have a penis, they develop a desire for a baby and turn to their fathers. Freud is not so clear why girls then begin to develop closer ties with their mothers. He suggested that the ties are not as profound and that a girl tries to identify with the mother, fearing that her mother will stop loving her. He called this equivalent complex for girls the Electra complex.

Parental influence

Interestingly, Freud accords parents significant responsibility in terms of how their children cope with each stage. Parents who over indulge their children by, for example, letting them suck their thumb constantly or not attempting to toilet train them and are then overly strict and force children to do things before they are ready, will create later personality problems for their children.

Erikson

Erikson was very much influenced by Freud's work, but considered that the social environment (e.g. parenting and friendships) also affected personality. He accepted Freud's theory of the structure of personality being divided into three – the id, the ego and the superego – but did not feel that Freud's work went far enough. His work is also interesting because he considered that our personalities are not fixed, but rather we keep on changing during the course of our lives.

Erikson's stages of personality development are life stages and are linked to social stages. He considered that at each stage we face a dilemma or conflict and that, like Freud, the outcome of each stage will determine our personality. The stages are summarised in Table 2.2.

Table 2.2 **Erikson's life stages**

Age	Dilemma	Stage	Effects on personality
0–1	Basic trust versus mistrust	Babies have to decide whether the world and the people around them are safe and friendly or hostile and to be feared.	If babies do not have their needs met, they may decide that their world is a place to be feared. This can mean that they lack the feelings of trust that are essential in order to form close relationships.
2–3	Autonomy versus shame	Children are learning to explore their environment and develop some control over their bodies and bowel movements. They may try to do things independently, e.g. dressing.	If children are not given encouragement to explore, or are made to feel guilty about toilet accidents, they may feel ashamed and doubt themselves. This can mean that they are overly dependent on others later on.
4–5	Initiative versus guilt	Children are increasingly able to plan and carry out activities. They also need to learn about their gender role – similar to Freud's phallic stage.	Children need to feel that they are independent, although they also need to learn what the boundaries for their behaviour are. Too much control may result in a fearful, dependent child, whereas too little control may result in a child without any guilt or conscience.

continued ▶

Age	Dilemma	Stage	Effects on personality
6–12	Industry versus inferiority	In these years, children are comparing themselves to other children. Teachers and parents may stress achievement.	Children who experience failure and notice that they are not as competent in some areas as their peers may lose confidence and feel inferior. Children in this stage who meet only with success may become over-confident and lack humility and empathy.
13–18	Identity versus confusion	Adolescents need to consider their identity, sexual identity and also what they wish to become in the future.	Ideally, at the end of this stage adolescents have a firm idea of who they are and what they want to go on to do. If they have not worked through this stage they may drift.
19–25	Intimacy versus isolation	This age group may be considering whether to lead a single life or to find a partner to settle down with.	Adults must decide whether to form a couple or stay single. If this conflict is not resolved, they may find themselves unable to commit to a relationship.
26–40	Generativity versus stagnation	Adults are often having children or are developing their careers.	Adults need to find a way of having an impact on the future. If adults do not feel that they have an impact, or are achieving nothing, they may become bitter and resentful.
41 +	Ego integrity versus despair	Adults are considering their own mortality.	Adults are trying to come to terms with themselves. They may feel satisfied and accepting of themselves or they may feel depressed and bitter.

6–12: Industry versus inferiority

Up until this point, children are often given praise for trying hard and 'doing their best' by adults. Erikson believed that at this stage, children and young people learn that their parents and teachers now expect results, i.e. that they learn to read, write and do well in tests. Their personality will be affected by how well they cope with this new pressure and the extent to which their parents' love is dependent on the results they produce. Children who cannot meet the new expectations might come out of this stage feeling inferior and believing that they are not capable.

13–18: Identity versus confusion

For Erikson, 3–18 years of age is a time when young people have to carve out an identity for themselves that is separate from their family unit in order for them to join the adult world. Erikson believed that this process creates an 'identity crisis' as young people may be torn between the expectations of their parents and their own inclinations.

Erikson's work is of particular interest as he coined the term 'identity crisis', which he used to describe the state that some young people are in during their adolescence. In the teenage years, Erikson observed that young people have to forge a new identity that will reflect their sexual maturity and also their need to develop an occupational role. This term was used by Erikson to describe the change in identity that was occurring, and it is now frequently used to describe any difficulty that people have when they are undergoing significant changes in their lives that affect their personality. It is still widely used in connection with young people.

What does it mean in practice?

Matching the way children learn to their personalities

In their book, *Mindwatching*, the Eysenck brothers suggest that teachers should focus more on children's and young people's personalities when planning how to help children learn. They suggest that it is nonsensical to assume that all children will benefit from the same type of teaching. They argue that children and young people who show more introverted characteristics will benefit from more of a direct style of teaching, one that would usually be criticised as being passive, whilst the extroverted would benefit from a more 'discovery and active' type of learning.

To support their argument, they point to research that shows that extroverted children do well in their primary phase of education, but less well in the second half of the secondary phase (around the time young people are beginning to study for GCSEs). The opposite is true of introverted children. The Eysenck brothers suggest that this correlates with the type of teaching and learning style provided in the different sectors, i.e. primary schools providing more hands-on activities and changing tasks, and secondary schooling being more passive and paced.

Self-concept

Today most people recognise and use terms such as 'self-confidence' and 'self-esteem'. Expressions such as 'It's not good for his confidence' are commonplace. It is widely understood that children, young people and adults of all ages need a level of confidence to cope with a range of situations, events and changes.

For children aged 6–16, there are many challenges in their lives, such as changing school, taking exams and coping with puberty. It is therefore helpful for you to understand the process by which children and young people develop positive feelings about themselves and thus the strong self-esteem that accompanies this. A good starting point is to understand the terms that are used in relation to this area, particularly self-concept. This is the overall judgement that you have of yourself and it includes the components below.

- **Self-image or identity** This is your sense of what you are like and includes gender and physical traits as well as characteristics and abilities.

- **Ideal-self** This is your view of what you would like to be.

- **Self-esteem** This is the 'judgement' component of self-concept. A person needs to be satisfied with their self-image when compared to their ideal-self in order to have a positive self-esteem.

Building self-image

Self-image is an important component in self-concept and is also involved in the process of developing self-esteem. Most parents, teachers and adults agree that children, and particularly young people, have to explore their identity and learn about themselves. Although, in reality, the process of exploring self has been under way since birth.

The story so far...

Self-image in young children

By the age of 6, children have already developed a strong sense of self. At around 21 months, babies recognise themselves in the mirror and by the age of 2 they know whether they are a boy or a girl. From 3 years of age onwards they are also beginning to explore what it means to be a boy or girl and may show this through their choice of toys, clothes and even play activities.

The key feature of young children's sense of self is how certain they seem, which is often expressed in sayings such as 'I'm not a baby' or 'I am good at tidying up.' Some of the learning about self that children have done in their first six years is based on what has been said to them and sometimes we can almost hear what adults have said echoing back: 'I am tall.'

Children also learn about themselves through noticing the reactions they have elicited in others. A child who has been praised for looking after a younger sibling may start incorporating a nurturing role into their sense of self, whilst a child who has made their family laugh may take on the role of clown.

The development of self-image continues to be influenced by what is said to a child and the reactions of others but, in the primary years, a new process begins to emerge. Children increasingly start to notice how they are doing in relation to others of the same age. This comparison can be seen when children begin to talk about their skills, features and abilities but also comment on others. It is particularly noticeable in the school context, where we might hear children talk about how well they are doing at reading, but in the next breath mention how others are doing also. 'I'm on the green shelf, but a boy in my class, he's already on the yellow one.'

Many teachers find that the beginnings of this comparison are present with 6-year-olds, but they actually become very noticeable as children progress through the primary phase. Children start to notice who is first to finish their work or who needs help. Comparison in this way can, for some children, help them to feel positive about their competency, whilst others as a result may begin to develop feelings of inadequacy in some particular areas.

As children are also learning about themselves through the reactions of adults, some also learn whether or not they have met the expectations of a teacher or parent. This again begins to influence their feelings of competency. In the early days of schooling children learn that putting in effort is sufficient to gain attention and adult approval. As they progress through the primary phase they recognise that teachers start to focus more on achievement. Thus it is not enough just to have 'done one's best', because praise and recognition are often tied to actually finishing work or gaining a high mark on a test.

Issues – Testing and booster classes

Since the 1990s, children in England have been tested at 7, 11 and 14 years of age. The idea behind testing was to ensure that all children were being adequately taught the National Curriculum. But as the results are also used to measure a school's effectiveness, it is claimed that the tests put undue pressures on children and teachers.

In many primary and secondary schools, 'booster classes' are provided in order to help children achieve the next level in their tests. Whilst some argue that booster classes can help children by providing them with targeted support, others suggest that they can put pressure on children and make them feel inadequate.

1. Talk to two parents and two teachers about testing and booster classes.

2. Find out to what extent they feel that the tests are useful.

3. Do they believe that they may have any effect on children's self-identity?

Booster Primary

I am a 'booster boy'
I'm in the booster class,
I'm boosted every morning,
I'm boosted really fast…

I have a booster teacher,
we do our booster tests.
Booster on my jacket,
booster on my vest.

Yes, I am a booster boy,
I get to school at dawn
for extra special boosting
in the special booster form.

I do not mind being boosted –
people say it's right –
so I boost away in daytime
and I wet the bed all night.

Peter Dixon

Self-image and cognitive development

The development of self-image in the primary phase also has links to children's cognitive development. Whilst young children rely heavily on physical characteristics and other detailed 'concrete' definitions to talk about themselves, from around 6 years onwards children start to add in more generalised characteristics about themselves, such as what they like doing and whether or not they have friends.

When asked to describe themselves, some children at 6 or 7 years old will still be providing very separate

▲ 'I am Louisa. I don't like tomatoes, but I do like grapes. I like to have my friends round for tea and I like going there too. I like listening to CDs and watching TV. I like playing with Brats and Barbie. I like to play mums and dads. I like school on Friday because I have chips. I like school on a Wednesday too because we are on the climbing frame. My best friend is Gracie. I am in year 3.'

statements about themselves rather than trying to evaluate who they are. The example on page 46, written by a girl aged 7 years, shows this clearly.

By the age of 11 or so, children are increasingly talking about personal characteristics such as being 'chatty' or 'funny'. In terms of cognitive development, as we will see in Chapter 4 Cognitive development, this would be expected, as children from 6 or 7 years increasingly construct more abstract thoughts.

Developing self-image 12–16 years

In this next phase, the sense of self-identity is really taking off and young people are starting to gain a global sense of their identity. Whilst some mention of physical characteristics is still made, especially in the early teens, the tendency towards using personality traits, beliefs and abstract ideas continues. Increasingly, young people qualify their comments and are almost less certain of themselves, as they no doubt realise that feelings and behaviour can change according to the situation and the people around.

Below is a piece of writing from a young person aged 16. It illustrates quite well how hard it becomes for young people to define themselves. As we will see later in this chapter, this gives some authority to theories, such as Erikson's, that young people go through an 'identity crisis' in their teen years. The sample below also shows how young people consciously recognise that judgements are attached to characteristics.

'I am L–, quirky, apprehensive about life, independent, shy and awkward at times. I am positive, often daydreaming, care a lot about other people's opinions, over-imaginative, childish (in a positive way), think a lot about things. I am sensitive, creative, like things to be planned, critical, friendly, self-conscious and I like to be right. This is difficult because…I'm not sure what to write. I don't really know who/ what I see myself as. I know people are going to judge what I write.'

(Marie-Lise, aged 16)

This phase is also marked by the way in which young people continue to compare themselves to their peers in a range of ways, including physical and academic terms. The comparison does not stop just with peers. Young people are also comparing themselves to their own ideals and expectations of themselves (see the discussions on ideal-self later in this chapter, page 55).

Self-identity is, of course, affected by how well a young person feels that he or she is doing at school. In this age range, some young people come to the conclusion that they are academic, whilst others may have feelings of inadequacy. Poor performance in one subject appears to have the potential to spill over into other subjects, although this depends on its status. A young person who perceives maths as a high-status subject but is struggling may begin to perform less well in other subjects. Whether or not a subject is considered to be of high or low status is dependent on a number of factors, including the value given to it by parents, other adults and, of course, peers.

Observing theory

Ask three young people aged 12–16 to rank their most important school subjects, although stress that these may not necessarily be their favourites or ones that they have opted to take.

1. Which subjects appear to have high status?

2. Are these the subjects that teachers and parents are likely to value?

The role of adults in building self-image

We have seen that building self-image is a process, but one of the key points is to understand that others, mainly adults, provide the context for this development to take place. Children and young people are heavily influenced in their development by their responses.

▲ Young people learn about themselves from the way others behave towards them

Learning through observation

A key way in which children and young people learn about themselves is by watching the responses of others towards them. A young child who is usually greeted with a beaming smile and a cuddle begins to learn that he or she is 'loveable', whilst a child who is frequently ignored may not. As well as simply watching the responses of others, it is important here to note that children are also aware of body language, gestures and facial expression. This means that they can sense whether there is sincerity behind a smile.

Learning through listening

Another key way in which children and young people learn about themselves is through hearing comments that are made about them and the tone of voice that is being used. Those who frequently hear warm praise and acknowledgement about themselves or their abilities will learn that they are valued. Those who frequently hear negative remarks are likely to shape a more negative self-image. Even the tone of voice used when a child's name is called gives children a powerful message about the responses of others.

Whilst direct comments are powerful, so too are indirect ones, or remarks that are overheard. A child may be told by his teacher that he is trying hard and doing well in maths, but may then overhear the teacher talking to his parents about 'catch-up classes'. It is therefore important for adults to be aware of what they are saying in situations where children are around.

Comparison with others

As a child's cognitive skills develop further, we also see that they learn about themselves through comparison. Children aged 6 are often able to identify the 'best' readers in a class, or the children who get into the most trouble, and may use these as reference points for their own performance. Children who perceive that they are better than most others at reading may well view themselves as a 'good reader'. (Seeing how we do in relation to others is something that continues, of course, into adulthood!)

Self-comparison

In addition to comparison with others, children and young people also start to compare themselves to their own expectations and what they have already learnt about themselves. A young person, who does not see himself or herself as good at maths but then gets top marks in a maths test, will not necessarily believe they are now good at maths. They may pass it off as a bit of luck. If, however, they repeatedly come top of the class, this may change.

Gender concept

As part of developing a self-concept, children and young people build in a construction of what it means to be a boy, girl, man or woman. Gender concept is interesting to look at, as we can see that it influences not only children's play and friendships, but also self-esteem.

The story so far...

Gender concept up to 6 years old

By the age of about 2 years, most children can recognise a boy or a girl. They can also place themselves in either category. By 4 years old children have also learnt that gender is permanent. This concept is known as gender stability. It means that a child knows that, if a boy dresses up as a girl, he does not turn into a girl!

As well as this, boys and girls need to learn about the expectations that surround gender, which is sometimes referred to as sex role stereotyping. This process is well under way by the time children are 4 years old. When shown cards with equipment, uniforms or places, they readily assign them to women or men. When it comes to the actual behaviour that children display based on gender, we can see that play preferences about toys begins remarkably early. Many children under 2 years old have started to have play preferences for sex stereotyped toys, such as cars and trucks or dolls. In addition, friendship preferences begin to favour the same sex from about 3 years old.

Gender concept 6–11 years

Children in the lower end of this age range are very 'concrete' about what boys and girls are meant to do and be interested in. Play and friendship preferences often demonstrate this. Same-sex friendships are usually the norm, with boys and girls even actively avoiding each other.

The type of interactions and play also mirror children's perceptions of what it means to be a boy or a girl. Parents often notice and, it is argued, reinforce children's gender role concept. Parents will, for example, buy sex stereotyped toys and also be accepting of a boy who does not want to wear a pink T-shirt. Indeed it is interesting that boys can become very distressed if made to wear or do something that is associated in their mind with girls.

From 9 years onwards, there is some change in the way children view what it means to be a boy or girl. Whilst same-sex friendships and play preferences continue, attitudes change and children become more accepting of children who do not conform to their own expectations. In addition, by 8 or 9 years most children are also able to attribute certain traits as being either masculine or feminine. Interestingly, in cross-cultural research, traits such as 'strong' and 'bold' are universally attributed to men, whilst 'gentle' and 'caring' are attributed to women.

Gender concept 12–16 years

In this age range, young people are more likely to understand that traditional sex roles and stereotypes are based on cultural norms and so are not absolutes. This means that they are less likely to say that a boy who plays with a doll is doing something wrong, although they may comment that the boy is unusual. This does not mean that they have come to terms with gender concept on a more personal basis. Young people need to integrate their gender into their own identity and consider to what extent to adopt the traditional masculine or feminine roles and traits. In addition, adolescents will also be considering their own sexuality. Traditionally, masculine identity and roles are tied in with heterosexuality whilst the converse is true for femininity. If a young person is not attracted to the opposite sex, this may throw up difficulties about how to dress, behave and respond.

Parental attitudes towards exploration of gender roles

The way in which parents react when their children are exploring gender roles is interesting. Firstly, parents of both sexes seem to have less of a problem with their daughters engaging in traditional 'boy' activities or dress codes. There is, however, a significant shift when it comes to boys who dress up in girls' clothes or are interested in activities usually assigned to girls. Parents seem to be uncomfortable, markedly fathers who are likely to show disapproval of what they may perceive as 'girlishness'.

Gender role stereotypes

A key feature of gender concept is the way in which children and young people learn about gender role expectations. We have seen that children as young as 4 years old are not only aware that they are a boy or a girl, but are already associating some activities with gender. There are several theories that attempt to explain the processes through which this occurs.

Social learning theory

The social learning theory suggests that children will learn about what it means to be a boy or girl from the adults they are with and also from the media. They imitate behaviours that they have seen, reinforced by adults encouraging them to behave and play with toys that are consistent with their gender. Support for this theory comes from research, which suggests that children whose mothers work have less rigid sex role stereotypes than those whose mother acts as the traditional primary carer. Interestingly, there is research to show that adults interact differently with boys and girls according to what the adult believes their gender to be.

Gender schema theory

The gender schema theory suggests that children are trying to find 'rules' for what it is to be a boy or a girl. They develop over time a 'schema' about what they have to do in order to be a boy or a girl. The schema theory may account for the way in which, for a time, boys and girls are quite rigid and rule-like in their approach. They are simply looking for rules about 'what men and boys do' and 'what women and girls do'.

Differences between boys and girls

Boys generally have more rigid sex role stereotypes than girls. Could this be a result of clear expectations gained from adults and the media about what boys and men should be like?

Psychoanalytical approach – Freud

Freud suggested that young children began to identify themselves more closely with the same-sex parent as a result of what he called the Oedipus complex in boys and the Electra complex in girls (see page 40). Freud believed that young boys fall in love with their mothers, but are afraid of their fathers' anger, which might result in their being castrated. Boys, he argued, therefore decide to make friends with their fathers by copying them, rather than risk their wrath. For girls, a similar process takes place, but they are in love with their fathers. The resolution of the conflicts results in children actively trying to imitate their own gender.

Developing ideal-self

Because comparing ourselves to our own ideals is a major part of the self-concept process, it is worth considering how the 'ideal' is formed. How do children and young people gain a picture of their ideal in the first place? The answer to this is likely to be complex and with many influences.

The media

The media has some influence on children's, but especially young people's, self-esteem. The extent of this influence is hard to measure, but ask young people about role models they admire and many will cite a person they only know about because of the media, e.g. a sporting hero, model or actor. A testimony to the power of role models in young people's lives is the way that they are used to market products. Advertisers use the power of role models in the media to promote brands, e.g. a famous footballer may advertise mobile phones.

Parents

Parental expectations and attitudes have a strong influence on children and young people. Parents may praise or give attention to skills, qualities and achievements and in doing so show the child or young person that these are valued. A parent who is a sporting fanatic may ask their children about PE lessons, encourage them to join in sporting activities and go to watch them. Children may, therefore, learn that sport is a valued activity and one that they should try to do well in.

As well as directly learning through their parents' actions towards them, children may also do so by watching and listening to parents' responses in other situations. A child may, for example, overhear a parent talking about a younger brother's reading skills, or notice that a parent talks admiringly about another family member who is learning to play a musical instrument. In a similar fashion, children and young people also take on messages through a lack of response, praise or interest. A young person who comes home from school with a certificate for working in the library may learn that this is not valued if no one at home shows interest in it.

Influential adults

Most children and young people will have contact with adults other than their parents. These may be family relatives, sports coaches or scout leaders as well as teachers and playworkers. As with parents, they too provide children and young people with perceived expectations and influence value judgements. A young person who plays in a band, organised by a youth worker who they like, may develop an ideal with some similar traits to the youth worker.

Talking to children and young people about their heroes can help us to find out what characteristics are valued in others. Below are two examples of what young people have said.

On Freddie Flintoff – successful England cricket player:
'I like cricket and he is the best. I would like to be as good as him. He's also good-looking.'
(Toby, aged 12)

On Sydney Bristow – heroine in TV series 'Alias':
'She's pretty, strong and has self-confidence. She is also intelligent and is determined.'
(Marie-Lise, aged 16)

Interestingly, many children will cite people that they know of from the media. Boys are likely to choose men, whilst girls are likely to choose women. Whilst it might be expected that young people would choose teachers, as they are in close contact with them, many do not. Celebrity, good looks and success seem to be associated with other jobs!

1. Ask three children and young people between the ages of 6–16 to talk about their heroes.

2. Who do they like and where have they learnt about them?

3. What is it that they like about them?

4. Do they think that they could be like them one day?

Peers and siblings

We know that, from the age of 6 or 7, children start to compare themselves to others. They also begin to see that adults focus more attention on particular children and use the other children as their ideal. Thus a young person who believes that her art teacher likes her friend because she is good at drawing may want to become more like her friend. This can sometimes show in the way that young people start to imitate the handwriting, gestures and even fashion styles of other young people. In some families, children's ideals are partly based on siblings, especially if the siblings are perceived as gaining more attention from parents.

Building self-esteem

Self-esteem is that part of our self-concept that sums up our value. It is important to understand that, like all parts of self-concept, it is a process that takes place individually and internally. This means that, whilst adults might provide optimum conditions for children and young people to feel good about themselves, we cannot 'give' them self-esteem. They have to 'feel' it within themselves.

The model cited by Helen Bee in her excellent text *The Developing Child* is by Susan Harter. This model suggests that self-esteem is a result of a child or young person comparing their self-identity to what they would like to be like – their ideal-self. Children and young people are, in effect, judging themselves by their own internal standards across a range of skills, relationships and situations. Self-judgements become increasingly critical. Whilst 6- or 7-year-olds are fairly positive about themselves, by the time children reach adolescence they are generally far harder on themselves. This is partly because young people's cognitive skills are more developed and so they are more aware of their abilities in relation to others.

Self-image *compared to* **Ideal-self** = **Self-concept**

Self-esteem – an internal and individual process

Whilst there are several influences on children and young people, it is important to remember that the ideal, used as a marker against which we judge ourselves, will be an individual one. This is because we are exposed to a range of different experiences, have different interests and, of course, different parents.

The process of measuring self-image against ideal-self is also an internal one. This explains why children and young people, who outwardly look as if they are confident and have nothing to worry about, may have feelings of inadequacy and low self-esteem. It is also important to understand that children and young people may be interpreting remarks, comments and responses of others in unintended ways. A parent may say to their child, 'You did quite well with that science work', and intend this to be a positive remark. The child may, however, perceive this as a signal that the parent is not satisfied because of the qualifying word 'quite' in the sentence.

Let us take the following scenario as another example. Michael is 12 years old and is going camping and abseiling with his school. The weather forecast is poor and his mother has been worrying about whether he will manage the rucksack, whether he will get wet or even be injured. This has resulted in 'tetchy' behaviour from her. On the day of the trip, she drops him off and does not stay like the other parents to wave goodbye. This is because she cannot bear to see him go and finds it easier to cope this way. She has always been like this and used to virtually push him through the door of the nursery rather than have a drawn out goodbye, especially if he was clingy. Michael goes over to his friend and mutters, 'My mum couldn't wait to get rid of me'.

THE TIMES TUESDAY MAY 24 2005

The things that wipe the smile off young boys' faces

by Tosin Sulaman

Teenage boys are now so obsessed with their appearance that a quarter of them would consider plastic surgery to achieve the looks and physiques of their celebrity heroes.

A study of 2,000 boys with an average age of 15 indicates that they agonise about their bodies as much as teenage girls do and envy David Beckham's six-pack or Brad Pitt's smile.

Just 13 per cent are happy with their bodies, while 26 per cent say they would consider cosmetic surgery. The most sought-after procedures mentioned were liposuction, penis enlargement and a nose job.

At Spungin, the founder of raisingkids.co.uk, a parenting website, said that she was not surprised by the findings because society was becoming more preoccupied with looks. "It's a change, because usually in the past this has not been an issue for young boys," she said. "Young boys have not been evaluated on the way they look in the same way. We appraise men now as we do women."

The survey, commissioned by *Sneak*, a teenagers' magazine, reveals the extent to which young boys' self-confidence is tied to their body image and how concerned they are about impressing girls.

Around 84 per cent of the teenagers believed that a better body would improve their life. They said that pressure from girls (42 per cent), celebrity pictures (28 per cent) and comments from other boys (24 per cent) had led to their loss of self-esteem. The findings also suggest that the growing market for male beauty products may be partly because young boys are taking more interest in their appearance. Nearly three quarters said that they would use moisturiser, fake tan and hair dye.

Dr Spungin said that the influence of football stars such as Beckham could explain the changing attitudes. "In a previous generation he would have been lauded for his talent. Now he is extending his brand to encompass his appearance," she said. "It's not enough to be an ace footballer. You have to be a good-looking ace footballer."

Male concerns	
Chest definition	68%
Teeth	68%
Legs	68%
Arms	67%
Bottom	65%
Penis size	64%
Face	62%
Hair	49%
Feel depressed about their looks	76%
Worry about their body shape at least twice a week	60%
Worry about their body shape daily	28%

Research it!

The article above suggests that boys are becoming increasingly concerned about how they look. In theory this should affect their self-esteem. Find out by talking to young people and their parents whether or not this article is correct. Are retailers responding to this supposed change?

The importance of self-esteem

Self-esteem plays an important part in the behaviour, choices and achievement of children and young people.

Making choices

Children and young people are most likely to do things that reinforce their own image of themselves and this, in turn, influences what they do. For example, children who believe that they are good at sport are more likely to join in team games and new sports, whilst children who do not believe that they are the 'sporty type' may not consider even trying.

As children develop, so their self-esteem will have an increasing impact on what they do when faced with choices. A young person who feels that he or she is 'academic' is more likely to choose subjects that reflect confidence in their abilities. Of course, a young person's feelings about the teacher of a subject have an influence here, as well as their own performance when measured against peers and self-expectation.

Effort

The amount of effort that we put into anything is partly determined by whether or not we feel that we can achieve success. Here again self-esteem comes into play. Children and young people who have strong self-esteem in relation to what they are doing are more likely to persevere and put in effort. As practice and effort are often key to mastering many skills, not putting in sufficient effort can result in failure, thus reinforcing low self-esteem and leading to a vicious cycle.

Behaviour

Some aspects of behaviour can also be linked to self-esteem. Children and young people who think of themselves as being 'good' are more likely to follow the behaviour codes of their parents and school. The converse can be true for children and young people who have learnt that their role is to be 'disruptive' or 'challenging'.

What does it mean in practice?

Discipline and behaviour

It is generally accepted that positive discipline is a good approach when working with children and young people. This means emphasising what behaviours are acceptable and looking to reinforce those. It also means avoiding personalising poor behaviour, so that children and young people do not assume that they are 'bad' or 'naughty'.

High expectations in terms of behaviour also seem to pay off. Children and young people who feel that adults trust them to behave well are more likely to show acceptable behaviour. This means that a more collaborative, rather than authoritarian, approach to setting boundaries and expectations works well. Children and young people are often able to set their own boundaries and talk through the implications of not adhering to them. Adults who encourage children and young people to do this are likely to find that those standards are very high.

Relationships

Our relationships with others are partly determined by who we perceive ourselves to be. Children, and especially young people, will start to be attracted to friendship groups on the basis of being accepted (see page 73 for more about friendship). Low self-esteem sometimes results in children and young people being dominated by a 'friend', as they may not see themselves as being equal or strong (see page 85 for more about bullying). In later life, low self-esteem is often cited as a reason why people stay in intimate relationships that have become abusive. As the dominance continues, this further lowers self-esteem.

Interview – *Betul, 12 years old*

Q. Have you ever had a friend who dominated you?

A. When I was 11, I had this friend who was meant to be my best friend. She wasn't very nice to me, although I didn't really notice at the time.

Q. What would she do?

A. She would call me names, and if I had something that she liked she would try and take it from me. I was a bit scared of her and she almost controlled me. I wasn't allowed to play or be friends with other girls, but she would go off and play and leave me alone. Once on a coach trip, I ended up sitting by myself because she said she would be my partner and then sat with another girl. It took a while to see that she wasn't really my friend.

Depression and low self-esteem

There is a significant link between depression and low self-esteem, although it is not clear whether low self-esteem causes depression. Depression amongst children and young people is considered to be on the increase. Speculation as to the cause includes pressure put on children and young people by media images, as well as increased testing in schools.

Stability of self-esteem

We have seen that self-esteem can have significant effects on children and young people. So is self-esteem something that is, in some way, fixed? This seems not to be the case. Firstly, scores for self-esteem in children aged 6–11 seem overall to be fairly stable, but there tends to be a downward dip during adolescence. This is probably to be expected, as young people aged 11 onwards have to come to terms with a changing body shape and changing expectations from adults around them. They are also in the process of moving from childhood into adulthood.

Raising self-esteem

It is important for adults working with children and young people to realise that there is no 'quick fix' when it comes to helping raise self-esteem. Children and young people will need long-term reassurance, support and evidence of improvement in order to be able to readjust their view of themselves. A single piece of homework with a better mark or a flattering comment may be welcomed but will not have the effect of changing core beliefs.

Many adults working with young people with low self-esteem report that positive comments are often met with some resistance and even hostility. This would make sense as the positive comments are actually challenging the young person's view of themselves and this makes them uncomfortable.

Gender differences in self-esteem

In young people there are some differences in self-esteem by gender. Overall, boys have higher self-esteem scores. This may be linked to the way in which masculine traits are often more valued than feminine ones. Teenagers, both boys and girls, who rate themselves as having a significantly higher proportion of masculine traits, tend to have high self-esteem. It could also be argued that girls today have to reconcile competing and conflicting demands, i.e. beauty, gentleness and femininity versus independence, assertiveness and strength, the latter traits being traditionally masculine ones.

▲ Do girls face more pressures than boys?

What does it mean in practice?

Countering low self-esteem

The way in which self-esteem develops means that children and young people with low self-esteem will need repeated successes for the view they have of themselves to change. This means that a long-term approach needs to be used with a child or young person who is identified as having low self-esteem.

It is also important to help children and young people evaluate areas in which they are not as successful as they want to be, especially where it is felt they are comparing themselves to others. Some children and young people internalise any failure, assuming that it is lack of ability rather than realising that other factors may be involved, such as lack of practice, poor equipment or sheer bad luck! We can sometimes help children and young people by acknowledging what they may be feeling and encouraging them to become more reflective.

Self-efficacy

Into the melting pot of factors that affect self-concept are children's and young people's feelings of 'self-efficacy'. This is a term first used by Albert Bandura to consider the extent to which we believe in ourselves. Those with a high sense of self-efficacy believe that they are capable and that they can have control over how well they do. This means that they may try out a new task, feeling that, if they work and practise hard, they should be able to manage it. Those without a strong sense of self-efficacy may start from the assumption that it might be too hard for them and that they cannot do anything about it. Strong feelings of self-efficacy are more likely to be gained where there is sufficient support, yet control over events and activities to ensure success.

What does it mean in practice?

Developing self-efficacy

Children and young people need to be given tasks, activities and responsibilities that will allow them to feel independent, successful and competent. Too many experiences where an adult comes and takes over because a child is not doing well will result in the child developing a poor sense of self-efficacy. Where children and young people have not managed to achieve a task, we should help them to evaluate the reasons behind this.

Issues – Young people and self-harm

Self-harm covers a range of behaviours that includes cutting, burning and hair-pulling. It is linked to emotional distress and over the past few years it has been significantly on the increase in the UK. In fact, the UK now has some of the highest rates of self-harm in Europe amongst young people. Some research suggests that 1 in 10 teenagers may self-harm, with girls more likely to self-harm than boys. Accurate statistics are hard to formulate as many self-harmers will not seek help or require medical attention.

Young people who self-harm often say that it is linked to an unhappy situation that they cannot control, such as a problem at school, bullying, divorce of their parents or feelings of depression and low self-esteem. Self-harming is not to be confused with attempted suicide, as the intention of the young person who self-harms is to make themselves feel better, not to kill themselves. Making yourself feel better through self-harming can be hard to understand, but young people say that it helps them to feel in control. Self-harming is something that young people tend to do in private and adults may not even be aware that it is happening unless medical attention is required. Self-harm should not been seen as attention seeking behaviour, as often the young person may not want others to know about it. It can, though, be a sign that a young person feels neglected and isolated.

If you suspect that a young person is self-harming, it is important not to panic, but to offer support. Criticism or anger about the self-harm may actually create the need for the young person to continue. Many young people use self-harm as a way of coping at the time, but may find that after a period they no longer need to continue. Many self-harmers do not know that this is a common phenomenon, so letting them know that there is support available can in itself help them to feel less isolated. Many organisations, such as the NCH (the children's charity) and Young Minds have information specifically written for young people. Links to their websites and to others dealing with self-harm have been made available at www.heinemann.co.uk/hotlinks. Enter the express code 983XP.

Attachment

As part of emotional development, it is important to look at the notion of 'attachment'. Whilst much of the attachment process is set down in early childhood, the effects of attachment are seen throughout childhood and into adulthood. In this section, we will look not only at the nature and theories of attachment, but also the importance and effects of the attachment process.

What is attachment?

Attachment is the bond that babies and children have with their primary carers, which usually means one or both of their parents. It is a unique bond because of its depth, strength and intensity, but also because of its length. Parents report that they still worry about their offspring even when their 'children' are middle-aged!

'I still worry about John, even though he doesn't realise. I always worry if he is eating properly. There's no reason that I should worry about him really. It's funny isn't it? I still see him as a child. I still buy him little things like I did when he was small.'
(Frances, 91 years old, talking about her son John, 74 years old)

The importance of attachment

The quality and nature of the relationship or attachment to one or more primary carers seem to set the tone for future social relationships, both in friendships and later on with partners. In the section on personality earlier in this chapter (see page 30), we noted how many theorists emphasise the interaction between parent and child in terms of the way a parent may either strengthen or decrease the extent of their child's personality traits. Thus it can be argued that the attachment process has a place in the development of personality.

The story so far...
Attachments formed by babies

Psychologists have studied the ways in which babies form early attachments. It is generally accepted that, unlike geese which immediately start to follow the first creature they see after hatching, babies form attachments gradually. There seems to be a general pattern to the way these develop and Table 2.3 summarises the stages.

Table 2.3 **Stages in formation of attachments by babies**

Age	Stage	Features
6 weeks – 3 months	Indiscriminate attachments	Babies begin to be attracted to human faces and voices. First smiles begin at around six weeks.
3 months – 7 or 8 months		Babies are learning to distinguish between faces, showing obvious pleasure when they recognise familiar faces. They are happy to be handled by strangers, preferring to be in human company rather than left alone, hence the term 'indiscriminate attachments'.
7 or 8 months	Specific attachments	At around 7 or 8 months, babies begin to miss key people in their lives and show signs of distress, e.g. crying, when they leave the room. Most babies also seem to have developed one particularly strong attachment, often to their mother. Babies also show a wariness of strangers even when in the presence of their 'key people'. This wariness may quickly develop into fear if the stranger makes some form of direct contact with the baby, e.g. by touching them.
From 8 months	Multiple attachments	After making specific attachments, babies then go on to form multiple attachments. This is an important part of their socialisation process.

Attachment behaviours: still present 6–16!

Attachment behaviours are seen frequently in babies and young children, but are still present throughout childhood and adolescence. The difference seems to be that, by the time children reach 4 or 5 years old, they are no longer being exposed to so many new situations. They have also developed a concept of their primary carer being available for them, and so do not constantly need to check that they are there. Times when children and young people will show attachment behaviours will be when they are distressed, ill or are having difficulties. These include:

1. actively seeking to be near the other person
2. crying or showing visible distress when that person leaves; showing joy or relief when that person appears
3. acute awareness of that person's presence, e.g. looking up at them from time to time.

▲ Strong attachment to parents is a major factor in emotional development

Q. Can you think of a time when you really needed one of your parents to be there for you?

A. Last year I went on a school trip. I had a lot of my friends with me and we had a great time. But when I fell down and badly hurt my leg, I really wanted my mum to be there. She would have known what to do. Even though everyone was really kind and nice, it wasn't the same.

Quality of attachments

Attachment is a two-way process. Parents develop an attachment to their babies, while babies attach to their parents. The way in which parents respond to their babies and toddlers seems to be quite crucial. Susan Ainsworth and her colleagues (1978) created a scenario by which babies' reactions to being left with a stranger and then reunited with their mothers (and/or fathers) was measured. This scenario is now widely used to study attachment behaviour and is known as the 'strange situation'. It is divided into eight parts with each part lasting about three minutes. During the experiment, the baby (approximately one year old) has some time alone, as well as with a stranger. The eight parts of the experiment areas follow.

1. Parent and baby enter the room.

2. Parent remains inactive; baby is free to explore the room.

3. Stranger joins parent and baby.

4. Parent leaves the room.

5. Parent returns, settles baby and stranger leaves.

6. Baby is alone in the room.

7. Stranger returns and interacts with baby.

8. Parent returns again and stranger leaves.

Ainsworth and her colleagues were particularly interested in the reactions of the baby to the parent when they left or returned, and the way in which the parent interacted with the baby. They categorised the behaviour into three types, as listed in Table 2.4.

Table 2.4 'Strange situation' behaviours

Type	Category	Behaviour
A	Anxious-avoidant	Baby largely ignores parent and shows little signs of distress when parent leaves, continuing to play. Baby ignores or avoids parent on their return. Baby dislikes being alone, but can be comforted by stranger.
B	Securely attached	Baby plays while parent is present, but shows visible distress when parent leaves and play is reduced. Baby is easily comforted on return of parent and carries on playing. Baby cries when alone because parent is not there, but can be partly comforted by stranger. Reactions towards stranger and parents are markedly different.
C	Anxious-resistant	Baby is wary and explores the room less than other behaviour types. Very distressed when parent leaves and actively resists stranger's attempts to comfort. Wants immediate contact with parent on return but is ambivalent, showing frustration and anger alongside clinginess, e.g. wanting to be held but then immediately struggling to get down.

How the quality of early attachment affects children and young people

One of the reasons it is important to look back at earlier development is because it often affects what we see with older children and young people. The quality of attachments between parents and their babies seems to have long-term consequences. Firstly, there seems to be some stability over time in terms of classification. Thus a baby who was securely attached is likely to remain securely attached. The exception is when there is a serious trauma in a very young child's life, such as the death of a parent, divorce or abuse.

Secondly, the type of attachment may affect behaviours and future relationships, including friendships. For those who were securely attached, there are positive effects. They are more likely to have stable friendships, show positive behaviours, cope with change and show more independence. As children move into adolescence, the same picture emerges. They are more likely to have high self-esteem and be popular with their peers. Fortunately, the research so far suggests that the majority of children fit into this category.

Sadly, the outcomes for children who had insecure attachments, either 'anxious-resistant' or 'anxious-avoidant', are not so positive. They may have early sexual relationships, less secure friendships and relationships, and may also show antisocial behaviour.

An explanation for the long-term effects of attachment

One explanation for why the effects of early attachment persist comes from John Bowlby, whose work on attachment was pioneering. He suggests that early attachment helps the child to set out its own rules or patterns for future relationships. Thus a child who has been securely attached in early life is more likely to have developed a positive inner working model about relationships. Whilst at first, this working model was identified with one or two particular people, as children get to around 4 or 5 years old they generalise it and so have a set of expectations that they apply to others who they meet.

What does it mean in practice?

Helping children cope with changes

Some children find it easier than others to start off in a new school, class or club. One explanation for this might be their earlier separation experiences. It is common to find that some children and young people have a track record of finding changes easy from nursery onwards; others may have always found this hard.

It can, therefore, be useful to find out from parents how their children have fared in the past. Children and young people who have always taken time to settle in, or who have been very anxious, may need more reassurance, adult support and time. In situations when they are changing school, they may also benefit from additional visits or time getting to know other young people who will be there.

We have seen that attachment takes place in the first year of life, but it does not stop there. Parents remain important figures in their children's lives although attachment behaviours, which are very noticeable in the pre-school years, decrease in frequency. This means that children appear increasingly independent of their parents and can, for example, happily stay the night at a friend's house or go on a short school trip. For some parents and observers, it might seem that the role and importance of the parents have diminished. The reality is different, as the moment that children find themselves in some sort of difficulty the attachment behaviours are likely to reappear. An unwell 7-year-old is likely to need the comfort and reassurance of a parent, whilst even a 10-year-old, whose pet has died, may well seek out a parent for consolation.

The reason often suggested for why attachment behaviours are less evident is that the child now has an 'inner working model' and so has learnt that parents do not need to be constantly with them for the support to be available.

Attachment to parents in adolescence

Even in adolescence, attachment to parents remains important. Whilst many parents and their offspring report an increase in tension and conflict during this time, parents are still central for many adolescents. This is not necessarily shown by their interactions, as disclosure about feelings and events is often transferred to peers. However, when asked about those who are important to them, many adolescents will report that parents still remain core in terms of relationships.

The source of conflict in adolescence is interesting to look at. Firstly, the amount of conflict and the intensity seems often to be linked back to the type of parenting that young people have received. Parents who overall have been quite responsive and warm in their interactions seem to be rewarded with less hostility and conflict. On the other hand very authoritarian or distant styles of parenting seem to provoke more conflict.

It is usually suggested that conflict is linked to young people's need to establish themselves as individuals in preparation for eventually leaving home. Erikson's 'identity crisis' theory links to this notion. In addition, parents often unconsciously behave differently during this period. The increase in height, change of appearance and the emergence of sexual characteristics often changes the way parents interact with their children. They may have higher expectations based on the emerging adult physique of their offspring, which may not always be realistic.

They may also find it hard to accept that their young person spends more time with friends and communicates less with them. Issues of freedom, boundaries and independence also have to be resolved. This is probably why families that have been able to communicate effectively in the past find the transition from adolescence to adulthood an easier path.

Chapter **2** Emotional development

▲ Adolescence can be a time of conflict between children and their parents

What does it mean in practice?

Working with parents

As parents remain central to children's and young people's lives, it is important to work with them as they have a long-term role. Parents can also provide insights into the early influences on their children. They may, for example, recognise that their child has always had difficulty in adapting to new situations or has always found it relatively easy to find friends. Parents may be the first to recognise changes in their children and we need to create an environment where they can pass on this information easily.

Some parents, especially of teenagers, report that they have fewer opportunities to be involved with settings. Interestingly, in terms of overall development, young people seem to do better when their parents are able to give them support. Having said this, if you work with a young person, you may also need to consider their right to confidentiality, especially if the young person is seeking help that may be put in jeopardy by contacting parents.

There are many different pieces of research looking at the effects of divorce on families. In 1998, the Joseph Rowntree Foundation produced a report that summarised over 200 pieces of research. One might expect it to be relatively easy to predict the outcomes of divorce and separation for children and young people, but it is a complex area. One of the factors that appears to affect children and young people is the amount of conflict associated with the parents' relationship breakdown, and whether or not a subsequent step-family is formed.

In terms of the level of attachment to parents, this depends on the quality of the attachment before separation takes place, but also the amount of contact between the absent parent and the child or young person. Thus the attachment between an absent parent and a child might still remain strong, provided that there is sufficient contact and that the relationship itself is strong.

The Joseph Rowntree Foundation report also comments that children from separated families have a higher probability of negative outcomes. The reasons for this are likely to be complex and influenced by more than one factor. For example, the financial circumstances of the parent who has custody and the way in which the parents separated can have significant effects on the children. Children and young people who have been exposed to conflict before, during and after the separation are often more affected than those whose parents have separated more amicably. Emotional development will often be linked to any conflict that children and young people are exposed to before, during and after the separation. The report also dispels some of the myths associated with separation. One popular myth is that boys will be more adversely affected than girls. This appears not to be the case, although the types of behaviour that are shown might be different. Another popular myth is that the impact is linked to the age of the child. Again, this appears not to be so.

The report also revealed that children of separated families:

1. tend to grow up in households with lower incomes, poorer quality housing and greater financial hardship than intact families (especially those headed by lone mothers).

2. tend to achieve less in socio-economic terms when they become adults than children from intact families.

3. are at increased risk of behavioural problems, including bedwetting, withdrawn behaviour, aggression, delinquency and other antisocial behaviour.

4. tend to perform less well in school and to gain fewer educational qualifications.

5. are more likely to be admitted to hospital following accidents, to have more reported health problems and visit their family doctor more often.

6. are more likely to leave school and home when young, and are more likely at an early age to become sexually active, form a cohabiting partnership, become pregnant, become a parent and give birth outside marriage.

7. tend to report more depressive symptoms and higher levels of smoking, drinking and other drug use during adolescence and adulthood.

(Extracted from the Joseph Rowntree Foundation report Divorce and Separation: Outcomes for children 1998 Ref 6106)

Chapter 2 Emotional development

Show your knowledge

1. How does self-esteem affect self-concept?

2. Give an example of a 'nature' theory of personality.

3. What are the traits suggested by the 'Big Five' theory of personality?

4. Are boys more likely to be affected by separation and divorce than girls?

5. Explain what the term 'attachment' means.

6. How can an early secure attachment benefit a child?

7. How does the nature of the attachment between parent and child change over time?

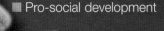

Chapter 3

Social development

Relationships with others have a significant impact on children and young people. Whilst at first young children rely on their parents as a major source of support, this changes over time, with children and young people developing their own networks of support. In Chapter 2 Emotional development we saw that interactions with others form the basis for self-concept, and so social development and emotional development are very much interlinked.

This chapter is divided into the following sections:
- Theory of mind
- The importance of friendships
- Bullying
- Relationships with adults
- Moral development
- Pro-social development

Theory of mind

One of the key ingredients in successfully making relationships is the ability to understand other people. Whilst children do learn through experience, there are also underlying development skills involved. Social development is therefore linked to other developmental areas, especially cognitive, language and emotional development.

The ability to understand what other people might be thinking and how this translates into their actions is sometimes referred to as 'theory of mind'. Children who have a good rate of development of theory of mind are likely to have good social skills. They are able to work out why another child might demonstrate a particular behaviour, but also predict how other children might react to their actions. This requires a good level of cognition and also language skills, so children whose development in these areas is atypical might find it harder to develop relationships.

Children with autistic spectrum disorder are thought to have a deficit in terms of theory of mind. They cannot imagine what other people might be thinking. They can only talk about what they are feeling.

Observing theory

The two photographs below are of Jeremy. In one photo Jeremy is smiling and is clearly happy. In the second he is looking sad. Show a child the two photographs. Check that the child knows that one represents happy and the other sad and then set the following scene:

Jeremy is at school and is playing happily with his friends. At home, his mother steps on and breaks Jeremy's favourite toy. Ask the child to decide which of the two photographs shows how Jeremy is feeling right now.

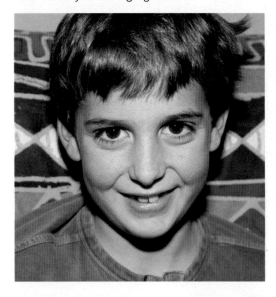 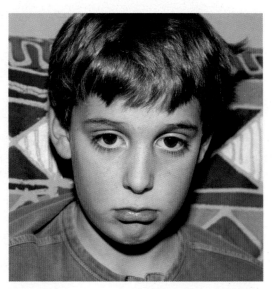

The importance of friendships

Whilst children and young people need their parents, they also need to learn how to make and sustain relationships with others. The starting point is the development of friendships with children of the same age and it usually begins when children first go to nursery or pre-school. But this is often not a smooth and painless process. Unlike family members, others do not have the child's interests at heart and will have different codes, values and behaviour models. Conflict and rejection, as well as security and happiness, tend to be features of this process. Not surprisingly, friendships can impact on other areas of development, such as academic achievement and self-esteem.

The story so far...
Development of friendships in very young children

For the first three years of life, most babies and children use adults or older children as their playmates. They may even show jealousy towards other babies or toddlers. In this period they are learning the basic skills of interaction, such as eye contact, facial expression and gesture. But at around 18 months, they may become interested in what other children of their age are doing. This means that a toddler might well play happily alongside another toddler and even make eye contact, but may not engage actively in play. This type of play is known as 'parallel play'.

Most young children begin actively to play with other children of the same age at around 3 years old. Playing with another child is often referred to as 'cooperative play'. This requires quite sophisticated skills that are associated with cognitive and language development. Examples of these skills include being able to take turns, share and negotiate. Developmentally, this is an enormous task. It means that children have to control their impulses by understanding that, for example, by waiting they will gain more pleasure.

In addition, children also need to have acquired sufficient language and communication skills in order to be able to understand what other children want, and read their body language and gestures. It is therefore not so surprising that physical squabbles and tussles are a feature of young children's play! Once the ability to play co-operatively has developed, the beginnings of friendships can be seen. By the time most children begin school at 4 or 5 years old, they will have a preferred playmate who, in the majority of cases, will be the same gender as themselves.

▲ Single-sex friendships are often seen in young children

Friendships 6–11 years

As we have seen, whilst young children will often prefer their parents' company over that of a friend, this starts to change as children become older. The role of friends in their lives becomes increasingly important. This can be seen in the way that, over time, the number of children that a child names as being their friend tends to increase. A 6-year-old may have only one or two preferred friends, but a 10-year-old may name four or more. (It is worth noting though that some children who are named by a child as a friend may not in turn name him or her.) The increasing importance of friends is also reflected in the amount of time that children spend with them and also their distress if they are having difficulties in making friends.

The nature of children's friendship in this phase is also interesting to look at. A good starting point is the way in which playmates are chosen, which is mostly linked to play interests and activities. Children who are friends are likely to talk to a parent about what they do together, rather than what their friend is like. This gradually changes over time, but it may account for the way in which children's relationships can be fluid, especially in the first couple of years of primary school. An 8-year-old may have a 'best' friend, but this will not stop him from playing football with other boys if his best friend has decided to attend a chess club that he is not interested in.

The link between play interests and friendships may be linked to children's cognitive development. Attitudes, values and feelings of loyalty are abstract concepts, whilst playing a game of chase is concrete or 'evident' and so may link to the stage of development of a child of primary school age. (See also Chapter 4 Cognitive development.)

'My friends are Kayleigh and Jasmine. Kayleigh I play with at school, but Jasmine I play with at home. I like playing with them.' (Sophie, aged 8)

'My friends are Byron, Aran, Will and Matthew. Byron and Aran will always help me. Matthew sticks up for me if there are bullies. Will is nice. The best thing about friends is that you can trust them.' (Jake, aged 10)

Observing theory

Talk to four children aged 6–11 years. Ask them about their friendships and why they like being with their friends. Notice the different ways they talk about their friendships.

▲ Friendships are important to children's happiness and well-being

Gender segregation

Whilst from 3 years onwards playmates are often chosen according to gender, this trend becomes very marked as children move through primary school. Not only do those of opposite genders tend not to play together, but they will often talk very negatively about each other, especially boys about girls. This is interesting to observe and there is some speculation that it is linked to the different play interests of boys and girls. Whilst there may be some truth in this, it does not account for the hostility, rather than simple indifference, that we can often see. Another possibility behind the separation of the genders is that boys and girls are still in the process of developing an understanding of gender identification and so are keen to associate with children of the same gender. Again, whilst this may be what is happening, it does not explain the strong antipathy that we can sometimes see.

When boys and girls do play together

There seems to be a set of invisible rules that temporarily 'allow' boys and girls, who normally do not play with each other, to do so. Firstly, it seems that it is all right to play with a member of the opposite sex or to work with them if an adult insists that you must, and in many primary classrooms, mixed groups of children do work together. But contrary to what the adults might hope for, few children then continue in their own time to carry on the play.

The gender divide can also be crossed if it is an older child playing with a much younger one. Thus playing with a friend's baby sister is fine, if you are a 10-year-old boy. In a similar way, children will also play with each other in the absence of any other children of the same sex. Thus a girl surrounded by boys at a social gathering may be invited into their game.

Interview – *Sophie, 7 years old*

Q. Do you play with boys when you are at school?

A. No. I don't play with boys. I do play with my baby brother at home though and Shaun sometimes. Shaun is in this school.

Q. Why don't you play with Shaun at school?

A. Because he is nasty to me and nasty to my friend.

Q. Is he nasty to you at home when you are playing?

A. No. He is different there. He plays there. At school he pushes and is rough.

Q. Do you ever play games with girls?

A. No!

Q. Why is that?

A. Because they are annoying. They come and poke us. They mess up our games.

Do boys and girls have different types of friendships?

Whilst it is important to avoid stereotyping boys' and girls' behaviour, it does seem that there are differences in their interactions and friendships. The terms 'extensive' and 'intensive', first coined by researchers Waldrop and Halverson in 1975, are now widely used to describe these differences.

Boys tend to be more competitive with each other, engage in more physical activity, particularly outdoors, and generally play in larger groups than girls. Thus 'extensive' has been used to describe these features, but also to include the sheer amount of space that boys might use in their play. By contrast, girls' interactions with each other are thought to be 'intensive'. Girls play in smaller groups or pairs and are often less welcoming when new girls want to join in. Their interactions are focused on cooperation rather than competitiveness and, in terms of the actual play, seem to require less space.

The reasons behind the differences are a source of intrigue and speculation. Again, as in other areas of development, the nature versus nurture debate comes to the fore! Are the different types of interaction modelled in some way or subtly reinforced by adults, or are they a result of innate differences between the sexes? Whatever the reason behind the differences between boys and girls, it is useful to remember that there are some commonalities as well. For a start, both boys and girls care about friendships and are keen to resolve differences. Both groups also plan and collaborate and show care for each other in their friendships. Thus a boy is just as likely as a girl to find an adult if his friend is hurt or upset.

Chapter 3 Social development

Observing theory

The school playground is often a fascinating place to watch children as they play. In the classroom a child may sit and work alongside another child whom they may not necessarily play with.

Watch children playing in a school playground.

- Can you see different friendship groups?

- Are boys occupying more space in their games?

What does it mean in practice?

Helping children to cooperate with each other

Many sensitive issues are raised in terms of anti-bias practice by children's preferences to play with children of their own gender. Adults must respect children's feelings but at the same time help children learn to cooperate with and respect each other.

- Organise activities that appeal to both boys and girls.

- Think carefully about competitions between boys and girls that may reinforce rivalry.

- Intervene if there is name-calling or insults are being traded.

- Make sure that resources and activities do not reinforce traditional gender stereotypes.

- Provide opportunities for boys and girls to work as team mates in structured or adult-led activities.

- Organise outdoor space and equipment in ways that do not prevent either boys or girls from enjoying it.

Why are some children more popular than others?

Some children in this age range seem to be more popular than others. They seem to attract other children to them in ways that some children do not. The reasons why some children seem to have a higher social status than others are useful to explore (see below). Outcomes for children who are repeatedly, and over a long period, rejected by others can be fairly negative. Some of these children may, in adolescence and adulthood, show antisocial behaviour and depression.

'I hate it when they choose a person to pick teams. They choose all their friends first and then everyone can see that you haven't got any.' (Stephanie, aged 14)

Factors that decide popularity

There are several factors that might affect the popularity of children. Firstly, and somewhat unfairly, children seem to be attracted to others who are physically attractive. This may be an innate factor, as studies of young babies also show that they will spend longer studying attractive faces than unattractive ones. Size also plays a part, with popular children often being taller than their classmates.

This is not the whole story though. Popular children also exhibit behaviours that are attractive.

- They are 'smiley' children who are helpful and supportive and, most importantly, non-threatening to others.

- They communicate well and use language rather than aggression to get their points across.
- They are able to control their emotions and can read other children's body language well.

Rejected children

Rejected children are those who are actively avoided by others. A feature of rejected children can be their tendency to be aggressive, hostile or take over other children's play. They may have poor language skills or find it hard to understand other children's feelings. Rejected children can get into a cycle of becoming more aggressive as they may retaliate when they find themselves being excluded.

Neglected children

Some children are simply ignored by other children rather than being actively rebuffed. Outcomes for neglected children can be quite positive, if their social skills are otherwise fine. Sometimes neglected children do not seek friendship from others and may be happy in their own company. Other neglected children may simply be shy and may not show through their body language, e.g. smiles, that they wish to be with others. For many children, simply changing the group of children that they are with can make a difference – a child who was once neglected can find themselves becoming popular.

▲ Rejected children are ignored by others and may play alone

What does it mean in practice?

Identifying children who may need support

Traditionally, there has been a laissez-faire attitude by people who work with children towards friendships but, as they are so important in children's lives, it could be argued that adults ought to be proactive in helping children to make friends. To do this we need to be able to identify children who may need extra support. Table 3.1 explores some features that influence popularity.

Table 3.1 **Features that influence popularity**

Feature	Relevance
Language	Children whose language and communication skills are not developed may find it harder to break into friendships. Working on these skills as a priority may therefore be beneficial.
Physical appearance	We have seen that attractiveness does play a part in popularity. For example, a child with a skin condition may be more vulnerable to rejection. It is important to take action therefore to support such children and also to help others learn not to discriminate against them. 'Persona dolls', for example, can be used to help children explore their attitudes and to think about others' feelings (see page 81). The way we act can also make a difference as children do notice adults' reactions towards others. Thus holding hands with a child with eczema will not only make the child feel valued, but also sends out a powerful message to the others about the value of that child. Personal hygiene also affects attractiveness. This is a sensitive area but we can, for example, provide tissues and encourage hand washing within settings. Talking to parents about hygiene requires a very skilful approach.
Shyness	Children who are slightly shy may need reassurance and might shine in more structured situations. Adults can help these children by thinking about the type of play activities provided, e.g. board games for two players.
Aggression	Aggression is clearly a turn-off when it comes to making friends. Thus a child who uses aggression is likely to be rejected by others. Causes of aggression can be complex and will need to be explored. Some aggression is linked to the aggression that children have experienced at home, whilst some children react to being rebuffed by other children by deliberately sabotaging a game or hitting out. Simply telling a child not to be aggressive rarely works, but providing opportunities for children to play in more structured ways, with adults or older children providing feedback, can be helpful. Some acts of aggression are also linked to children simply not understanding the intentions of others, e.g. they may believe that a ball was thrown deliberately at them. Providing children with a commentary and feedback can be helpful.
Other differences	Children whose culture, dress, first language or learning ability is different from their peer group may be vulnerable to being unpopular. Again, adults need to be proactive with the other children. Settings with a good anti-discriminatory policy, which transfers to the actual provision, tend to do well by these children. Resources, activities and the way of working reinforce the importance of valuing everyone.

Persona dolls can help children to be inclusive

Persona dolls are special dolls used with groups of children to approach sensitive issues, or to help children talk about feelings. A doll takes on the 'persona' of a child in the setting where it will be used. It will be given an age, name and family history, and may also have pets, interests and other things that the children can relate to. Once introduced to the group, an adult can tell the doll's story and speak for it, letting the doll talk about specific issues that the adult feels will be helpful. Thus if a child has been excluded by others, the persona doll may tell the children about the time when it had no friends and what this felt like. Learning from another 'child' can help groups of children to modify their behaviour, and many teachers and other adults working with children find using persona dolls extremely helpful. Note that persona dolls also talk to children about happy events, which ensures that the doll has a balanced persona.

Buddying systems

Many schools now recognise the importance of friendships in children's lives and the unhappiness that children can feel if they do not have anyone to play with. This means they are actively looking for ways to help children.
A system that has some success is a 'buddying' system. Children volunteer to act as 'buddies' and when other children find that they have no one to play with, they go to a designated place where the buddy will play with them. Buddies may also be on the lookout for children who look lonely. Buddies often wear a badge, waistcoat or something else to identify them.

'Sometimes I come to school and I can't see any friends to play with. It's not a nice feeling and I feel sad. I then have to go round to other boys and see if they will let me play. Sometimes they do, but sometimes they won't. You can go to the bench if you have no one to play with. I have done it and you can find someone there to play with, but it's not the same as playing with your friends.' (Jake, aged 11)

Friendships 12–16 years

Between the ages of 12 and 16, there are significant changes to the patterns and nature of friendships. Young people have more reciprocal friendships, now based on traits rather than activities. This means that a young person may talk about their friend as being 'nice' or 'fun' rather than focus on the way in which time is spent with them.

Friendships, which were already important for children, are now a major influence in young people's lives. Time spent with friends increases dramatically and many young people will spend longer in the company of their peers than they will with their family. Friendships are also likely to last for significant amounts of time and some will, of course, become life-long.

Whilst gender segregation was the norm in the younger age group, gradually mixed groups take over. This represents a significant change, but it is worth remembering that some young people will be attending single-sex settings and may not have the opportunity to be part of a mixed group.

Moving away from parents

Whilst time spent with parents decreases, the influence of peers increases. Young people use their friends and peers to develop further their sense of identity and to become independent. This is, of course, a major and normal task for young people but, not surprisingly, one that can cause conflict with parents. Not only do a young person's friends take over in terms of time, they are also the people with whom a young person shares most thoughts, anxieties and information.

This represents a change, as most children previously talked about significant and day-to-day events with their parents. Parents of teenagers tend to be given basic, if any, information, although as we have seen in Chapter 2 Emotional development, if young people are in any serious difficulties, such as being involved in an accident, they will still turn to their parents. Talking more to friends seems to be just the first stage in becoming independent. Later on, young adults turn to their partners to confide in.

Cliques and crowds

We have seen that friendships are based more on traits, interests and shared value systems in the teenage years. In addition, during this period the structure of groups undergoes some changes. Observations by Dexter Dunphy in the late 1950s and early 1960s resulted in the terms 'cliques' and 'crowds' being used to describe these changes. Dunphy suggested that, in early adolescence, same-sex cliques start to appear, where a clique is composed of 4–6 young people. Young people in a clique will have a strong bond with each other. It might be argued that this helps young people to make the move away from their parents as the clique may be acting as a surrogate family unit. Later on, when young people reach 13 or 14 years, cliques seem to combine to form 'crowds'. Crowds are likely to consist of both boys and girls.

Moving on

Whilst being in a crowd is extremely important at 13, it is far less important at 16. By this time, most young people are beginning to assume a personal identity rather than using the group one. Group sizes start to become smaller and young people are likely to go back to having a smaller circle of close friends. From this point onwards, young people are also likely to be moving into more intimate relationships and start to become 'pairs'. Whilst, overall, friendship tends to follow the pattern described earlier in this section, some young people have a partner in their early teens. Whilst this relationship may become an intimate or even sexual one, the young person may still not leave their 'crowd'.

Peer group pressures

A well-known feature of young people's relationships is the way in which they tend to want to 'fit in' with each other. A young person's sense of identity is almost transferred away from the family unit and towards a group. Groups of young people may wear similar clothing, or be interested in the same music and activities. Fitting in with the group becomes important for many young people, particularly 13- and 14-year-olds.

Many parents will blame a young person's friends for their behaviour or, say, lack of interest in schoolwork, and it is common to hear the phrase, 'He's got in with a bad crowd.' This gives the impression that groups take young people prisoner. This is not the case, as, in reality, a young person will tend to be drawn towards a group of other like-minded young people. Thus a young person who is already finding schooling difficult is likely to gravitate towards others who are also less interested. However, once in a group there is a pressure to conform. Those whose own interests and inclinations change, or do not initially match those of the group's, tend to move towards other groups.

Whilst peer pressure is usually seen as negative, some peer pressure can have positive benefits. Being in a group gives young people tremendous support and feelings of validation. This is why it is an important step in terms of self-identity. The exception comes when young people who are aggressive or have antisocial tendencies come together. Instead of acting as a restraining influence, peer pressure in these circumstances can encourage more antisocial behaviour, especially amongst boys.

Who's who?

In secondary schools, a young person is likely to know what the different groups or crowds represent in terms of attitudes and values. Some crowds have more status than others and many will be named, for example 'the boffs' for those who are academic, or 'the grungers' for those who wear black and who listen to heavy metal music. With each crowd having a distinct identity, young people know the type of activities, behaviours and expectations that are associated with them.

'In our school there are about three different groups. There is the popular group. You can tell who they are just by seeing them. They wear their collars upright instead of down. They act hard and the girls wear lots of make-up. Then there are the 'keeners'. They don't wear make-up and are really quiet in class. They don't muck around. I am in the normal group. We don't get in too much trouble so we're in the middle.' (Rachel, aged 14)

'You can just tell who to steer clear of by looking at them. They may be really loud, but it's also the way they dress.' (James, aged 12)

▲ Young people can identify different crowds within a school by how they adapt their uniforms

Observing theory

Ask children and young people of different ages whom they talk to about things that happen at school. Do primary school aged children tend to disclose more to their parents than young people?

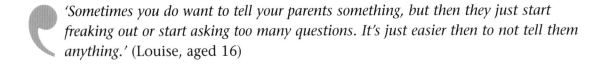

'Sometimes you do want to tell your parents something, but then they just start freaking out or start asking too many questions. It's just easier then to not tell them anything.' (Louise, aged 16)

Bullying

Whilst many adults would like to imagine that childhood is a happy time, this is far from the truth for those children and young people who experience bullying. The statistics surrounding bullying are fairly alarming, with most children at some time reporting that they have been bullied. Whilst bullying was once seen as inevitable, today there is an understanding that bullying has not just short-term, but also long-term consequences for the victims. In extreme situations, bullying has been responsible for young people taking their own lives. Therefore, tackling bullying has become a priority area for many schools and settings.

Types of bullying

Bullying can take many forms, ranging from physical aggression through to name-calling or being shunned. Statistics from the charity Bullying Online suggest that name-calling is the most common type of bullying experienced by children and young people of all ages and both genders. The latter may come as a surprise, as it is often thought that boys tend to bully using physical aggression rather than employing emotional strategies. Whilst adults may be inclined to dismiss name-calling as minor, for the child or young person involved it can affect their self-esteem and make their life fairly miserable.

Whilst name-calling is the prime way in which bullying takes place, aggression is also a tool, although more common in the 6–11 year age group and more likely amongst boys.

Statistics

One in five young people aged 11–19 said that they had been bullied or threatened via modern technology such as text messages, emails or in internet chat rooms. (Source: Mobile phone survey carried out by NCH and Tesco Mobile in 2005.)

Fifty-four per cent of primary and secondary pupils say that bullying is a 'big' or 'quite big' problem in their school. (Source: DFES, 2003.)

Frequency of bullying

Reports of bullying seem to decline as children and young people get older, but the severity and its impact does however increase. Children aged between 6 and 11 are more likely to have frequent fallings in and out with their friends, but these are often quickly resolved. With young people, there are fewer incidences, but it is important for anyone working with this age range to realise that they must not be trivialised. It is noteworthy that there are much fewer incidents of bullying amongst 15- and 16-year-olds. This may link to the way in which friendship groups have become smaller; but also potential victims might find it easier to avoid being with those who may see them as a target.

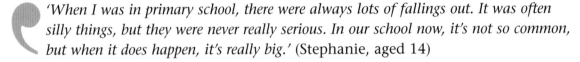

'When I was in primary school, there were always lots of fallings out. It was often silly things, but they were never really serious. In our school now, it's not so common, but when it does happen, it's really big.' (Stephanie, aged 14)

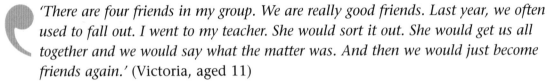

'There are four friends in my group. We are really good friends. Last year, we often used to fall out. I went to my teacher. She would sort it out. She would get us all together and we would say what the matter was. And then we would just become friends again.' (Victoria, aged 11)

Are some children more likely than others to be bullied?

Whilst some incidents of bullying are random, some children do seem more at risk of being targeted than others. Being aware of who these children and young people are may help us to protect and support them. Bullies tend to target children who are alone and do not have friends. We have looked at children who may need extra support in making friends (see page 80) and these same children may also become victims of bullying, if support is not provided. As having friends seems to be a protective factor, so schemes such as the 'buddy system' are particularly relevant.

Potential victims of bullying also seem to show more anxiety, passivity and have low self-esteem, and so become more vulnerable. This is likely to be exacerbated as a result of a bullying incident and so, crucially, may create a scenario where further bullying takes place. It is important here to emphasise that this does not excuse bullying behaviour, but it might give us some clues as to how best to help a child or young person who is experiencing bullying. Helping victims to regain confidence and gain friends may be an important tool in anti-bullying policies.

Some victims are also bullies

Whilst many children and young people say that they have experienced bullying, many will also admit that they have bullied others. This is one reason why bullying is such a complex issue. The organisation Childline, which supports children, found that 15 per cent of primary school aged children and around 12 per cent of young people reported both being bullied and also bullying others. Victims and bullies tend to be less popular, have fewer social skills, are easily provoked and good, too, at provoking others. This group may need help with their social skills and learning how to talk about their feelings.

Unnoticed bullies

Whilst some bullies are clearly recognisable by their behaviour, some go unnoticed by adults. These tend to be popular with adults and children, have good social skills and high levels of self-esteem. They may even have been previously good friends with their victims. This runs contrary to the image of bullies as always being loners and having low self-esteem.

The high self-esteem of an unnoticed bully is reinforced by the way in which they may have control and power over their victims. These bullies know what they are doing, but their victims may find it harder to report what is happening, given the bully's social standing.

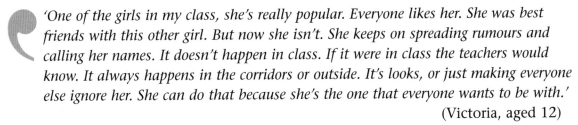

'One of the girls in my class, she's really popular. Everyone likes her. She was best friends with this other girl. But now she isn't. She keeps on spreading rumours and calling her names. It doesn't happen in class. If it were in class the teachers would know. It always happens in the corridors or outside. It's looks, or just making everyone else ignore her. She can do that because she's the one that everyone wants to be with.'

(Victoria, aged 12)

Group bullying

Many acts of bullying happen in the presence of other children and young people. Whilst only one or two may initiate the original bullying, others may join in or fail to support the victim. Where children and young people come together, bullying can grow in intensity and so has the potential to be more devastating in terms of consequences for the victim. Onlookers, or those who join in rather than actually initiating the bullying, may do this because they are learning that these acts are accepted and encouraged by the group. This is likely to be the social cognitive theory at work, with children who may otherwise have not acted in a hostile way noticing what others are doing and so joining in (see page 35). Onlookers who fail to help may also be afraid that they may be bullied for helping the victim. (See also discussions on pro-social behaviour on page 99.)

Reporting bullying incidents

Research carried out on reporting of incidents suggests that girls are more likely than boys to seek help, and so more incidents of bullying are reported by girls. In addition, there is a higher level of reporting amongst children aged 6–11 years. But not all children and young people who are bullied will report what is happening. Some believe that intervention by adults will make things worse for them. Others do not believe the adult will be able to help them. This can lead to great feelings of isolation and unhappiness. Fortunately, services such as Childline exist and do provide support, although sometimes there are limits to the support that can be offered from a distance. Sadly, Childline reports that many children and young people have already tried to report the bullying to adults, but have not been satisfactorily supported.

'When I first joined secondary school, there were some boys who were name-calling. It wasn't very nice. It wasn't just me that they did it to. We turned around and went to the head of year. It was a group decision to go. We were all nervous in case it would get worse. She was really nice. She spoke to them and they did stop. I think that my school is good about bullying. But the teachers can't be everywhere. They can't see the looks that people end up giving.' (Victoria, aged 12)

What does it mean in practice?

Recognising the signs of bullying

It is important to pick up on the signs of bullying as some children and young people, especially boys, may not feel that they can say anything. Signs to look out for include:

- not wanting to attend the setting or regularly complaining of feeling unwell
- being happier and more relaxed during holidays, weekends or when not required to go to the setting
- marked change in behaviour, e.g. moody, aggressive, tearful or withdrawn
- bedwetting, nightmares or difficulties getting to sleep
- cuts, bruises and small injuries that the child or young person is unwilling to talk about
- dishevelled appearance, torn clothing
- items that go missing that the child or young person would normally care about
- avoidance of conversations about friends, play times, etc.

If you do notice signs of bullying, it is essential to be extremely sensitive. Some children and young people may deny that it is taking place, as they may not be confident enough to seek help.

- Tell the child or young person that you care about them.
- Tell them that you suspect they are having difficulties and that these can be sorted out.
- Make it clear that being bullied is nothing to be ashamed about and that it is not their fault.
- Listen to the child or young person, if he or she wishes to talk about it.
- Try to find out where the bullying is occurring and who the perpetrators are.
- Encourage the child or young person to think about where they might get help or explain the procedures for doing this within your own setting.
- Provide the phone number of Childline (0800 1111).

Dealing with bullying

Whilst bullying is complex, this does not mean that settings cannot attempt to address it. According to Andrew Mellor, a researcher into bullying, three factors will influence a setting's success in dealing with it.

1. **Recognition** A setting has to openly recognise that bullying is an issue.

2. **Openness** It has to create a culture amongst children and young people that allows them to talk about what is happening to them.

3. **Ownership** Everyone, including parents, staff and the children themselves, must work as a community to address bullying.

No blame approach

There are several approaches to bullying that settings can take. One of the more innovative ways is called the 'no blame' approach. This is non-punitive and aims to help the bully and those associated with the bullying to take responsibility for their actions. It also recognises that the way to prevent further occurrences of bullying is to change the group dynamics and behaviour. This means that onlookers, as well as those who join in, are included in tackling the behaviour, rather than just the bully and victim.

- **Step one** The adult talks to the victim and finds out who is involved, including onlookers as well as those engaged in the behaviour.

- **Step two** A meeting is arranged with the people involved.

- **Step three** The adult explains the problem to the group and helps them to find out how the victim is feeling. At this point, the group may talk about the victim's behaviour towards them as well.

- **Step four** The group is told that they need to take responsibility and that they can do something about it. Each member of the group is encouraged to suggest a way in which the victim can be made happier and the situation resolved.

- **Step five** The adult listens to their plans and gives positive feedback.

- **Step six** The adult arranges to meet them again to see how things are going.

- **Step seven** After a week the adult discusses with each person, including the victim, how things are going.

Circle time

Circle time is another group approach to bullying, although the group size is not restricted to those directly involved. Circle time works by getting children and young people to talk about their feelings and the behaviour of others in a controlled situation. The aim is that each person can 'have a voice' without fear of interruption. Circle time is useful as a way of taking the stigma out of bullying by openly talking about it. The technique can also be used as a preventative measure. Circle time works particularly well with children aged between 8 and 16 years as this age range has usually developed the language skills they need to articulate their feelings and take responsibility.

Relationships with adults

As well as forming relationships with their peers, children and young people also have to interact with adults. One researcher, William Hartup, sees these types of relationships as being very different in nature. He refers to them as being 'vertical', as opposed to relationships with peers which he terms 'horizontal'. Hartup believes that children and young people need both types of relationships.

Relationships with peers, as we have seen, are usually on very equal terms. This is perhaps reflected in the way in which children and young people talk to each other and also the content of such talk. Relationships with adults are different in nature. Adults have more social experience, knowledge and skills, and so the relationship is not an equal one. Children and young people can learn from adults but also be supported by adults and this can be extremely positive.

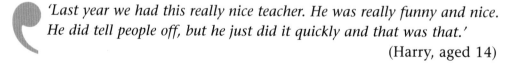

'Last year we had this really nice teacher. He was really funny and nice. He did tell people off, but he just did it quickly and that was that.'

(Harry, aged 14)

'I can't stand my maths teacher. I think it's because she singles me out and tells me off in class in front of everyone. She is often frowning. You get the feeling that she doesn't want to teach you. She's always angry. I definitely prefer the subjects where the teachers have smiley faces.'

(James, aged 13)

Communicating well with children and young people

◼ Take time to listen as well as to talk.

◼ Create situations and opportunities for one-to-one talking, e.g. whilst preparing snacks, tidying up.

◼ Acknowledge sadness and disappointment in the same way that you would acknowledge positive emotions such as happiness.

◼ When children and young people share problems, help them to work through their own solutions or reflections.

◼ Avoid being judgemental so that children and young people feel free to talk openly.

◼ Show through comments and facial expression that you enjoy being with a child.

◼ Remember that, in terms of social skills, you are acting as a role model.

Moral development

Moral development relates to the principles of knowing right from wrong, and is also about showing this in actions. Parents, teachers and other adults are keen for children to show 'good' behaviour and eventually be thoughtful and honest. This area of development can make a difference in terms of our expectations of children and young people.

When looking at moral development, it is important to remember that there is a big difference between knowing what should or should not be done and actual behaviour. This applies not only to children and young people, but also to adults. A good example of this is the way that most motorists agree that it is wrong to speed near a school, but quite a few still do so.

Morality can be affected by context

What seems to be perfectly fine in terms of actions and attitudes in one situation can be seen as totally unfair or immoral in another. We have seen this over the course of history. Today in the UK, we look back at times when children worked in mines or swept chimneys as being wrong, but 200 years ago this was not the case at all. Thus right and wrong are not set in stone and are the product of factors such as religion, culture and family context, as well as the influence of society at large.

The story so far...

Moral development in young children

Many theorists who have looked at moral development take the view that very young children are amoral. This means that they do not have any moral principles and are likely to act only in order to please adults or to prevent any negative consequences (i.e. punishment). This would mean that young children's thoughts about right and wrong are completely fluid and are guided by the adults that they are with.

Young children tend to focus on what will happen to them if they do something wrong rather than on the reasons why their act is wrong. Thus a 5-year-old may tear a page in a book belonging to another child and understand that he is in trouble, rather than thinking about the consequences of the act itself for the other child.

Theories of moral development

There are several theories that attempt to explain how young children move from being relatively amoral through to developing their own code of behaviour.

Psychoanalytical theories

In Chapter 2 Emotional development, we looked at Freud and Erikson. Both have theories about children's moral development, which suggest that children learn their moral code from and are influenced by their parents. According to Freud, a child's same-sex parent will have a significant effect on their morals. From around 3 years old, the child will start adopting their parent's moral rules, although significant development takes place later when the child develops a superego at around 6 years old. The superego is divided into two parts: the ego ideal and the conscience. They in turn are responsible for making children feel guilt and shame.

Whilst Freud emphasised the role of guilt and shame in moral development, Erikson differed slightly by considering the importance of pride. He suggested that it was important for children and young people to congratulate themselves internally when they had taken a 'right' action. Whilst Freud focused on learning morality from the same-sex parent, Erikson considered both parents equally important.

Are guilt and shame enough?

There is some speculation that feelings of guilt and shame may not be sufficient to change behaviour. Children aged 7 may feel guilt and shame, but only because they have been 'caught' and reprimanded. From around 9 or 10 years, children may resist temptations because they are able to predict how they will feel afterwards and want to avoid guilt and shame. Later, young people start to express shame as being upset with themselves for failing to live up to their own internal standards.

Observing theory

Ask several children of different ages: 'What does it feel like if you have done something wrong?' See whether their answers match the theories of guilt and shame.

Behaviourist theories

Behaviourist theories show us how children develop morals as a result of being with others. They explain why children may sometimes say one thing, but do something else in certain situations. It is worth noting here that using behaviourist models alone to support moral development will not help a young person develop their own internal moral code. As we will see from looking at Kohlberg's work (page 96), it is important to use discussion, reasoning and opportunities to explore issues.

Operant conditioning

Operant conditioning is a term that comes from studies that looked at the role of reward and punishment in shaping behaviour. Children learn that what they do may have consequences: taking turns and sharing may result in being given praise, whilst snatching may result in the toy being removed. This is operant conditioning.

Most psychologists emphasise the importance of rewards in shaping behaviour, as this seems to have greater long-term effects. Punishments, especially extreme ones, can actually act as a distraction. Shouting at a child may mean that the child focuses on the shouting rather than on their action. It also sends out a signal that shouting is acceptable behaviour. This is why behaviour policies always emphasise the need for adults to be calm.

Chapter 3 Social development

Social cognitive theory

Social cognitive theory suggests that children will learn about morality by watching other adults or children. A child who sees that another child has been rewarded for helping someone may copy this action in the hope that he or she will also be rewarded. In the same way, if a child sees an adult take something without paying, the child might learn that stealing is acceptable.

Whilst this sounds simple, in reality the learning of moral principles in this way can be more complex. Most adults, who tend to act as role models, are inconsistent. They may, for example, be patient in one situation but not in another. Children may also change their mind about how to act as a result of watching others. For example, a child may see some chocolates on a table and decide not to take one without asking. However, if they see other children doing so, they may copy them.

Other approaches to moral development

Behaviourist approaches to moral development do not deal with the way in which reasoning changes with age. Two theorists are particularly noted for looking at these changes: Piaget and Kohlberg.

▲ Has this child seen an adult help another child?

In Chapter 4 Cognitive development, we will look at Piaget's work in relation to cognitive development. Here we will focus on Piaget's experiments and conclusions about moral development. The two, however, are entwined.

As with his theory of cognitive development, Piaget's approach to moral development is in stages. Piaget used a clinical interview approach with children, asking them to explain how they were playing games, and he also told them stories. He suggested that children's moral development occurred in three stages: pre-moral, moral realism and moral relativism.

He was clear that very young children are amoral (the 'pre-moral' stage). Later, in the 'moral realism' stage, Piaget suggests that children feel that rules are somehow passed on from on-high and cannot be changed. This is perhaps why children in this stage get so worried if they accidentally break something. Their assumption is that there is no flexibility and that they will definitely be punished. This changes from around 8 years old when they enter the 'moral relativism' stage. Here, they are very focused on rules but they also see that rules can be changed to suit new circumstances. Another significant change in their thinking is the realisation that 'intention' is also important. Thus accidentally hurting another child is not the same as deliberately doing so. Sometime after 11 years, young people start to become aware that morality is not just doing what others expect of you, but about developing and following your own code or 'autonomous morality'.

Table 3.2 **Piaget's stages of moral development**

Moral stage	Age	Features
Pre-moral	0–4 years	Children have no morals but begin to learn about right and wrong through their own actions and consider those of adults around them.
Moral realism	4–7 years	Children's moral development is greatly influenced by the adults in their lives. Their judgements very much depend on what they think the adult's expectations would be.
Moral relativism	7–11 years	Children are preoccupied with justice and following rules. They have developed a concept of fairness and they also consider the motive for people's actions.
	11 years +	Children understand the concept of equity and that treating people in exactly the same way may not result in fairness, e.g. a child who does not understand their homework may need more of a teacher's time than a child who does.

Kohlberg's stages of moral development

Lawrence Kohlberg's stages of moral development have been hugely influential and are widely accepted. Kohlberg built on Piaget's work by creating a series of dilemmas which he used to see the moral reasoning that children, young people and adults were using in order to provide a solution. He concluded that moral development could be divided into three main stages with sub-stages (see Table 3.3). Note that Kohlberg did not have a moral stage for children under 6 years. This is because he, like Piaget, felt that very young children were not using any moral reasoning but merely reacting to adults. It is also worth noting that, whilst the table shows the ages at which different levels are reached, Kohlberg was clear that this development was not automatic. In subsequent research it has been found that many adults are in sub-stages 3 or 4.

Table 3.3 **Kohlberg's stages of moral development**

Age	Main stage	Sub-stages
6–13	Pre-conventional	1. Punishment and obedience 2. Individualism, instrumental purpose and exchange
13–16	Conventional	3. 'Good boy/nice girl' 4. Law and order orientation
16+	Post-conventional or principled	5. Social contract 6. Universal ethical principles

Pre-conventional morality

At this level, children are not being guided by their own moral reasoning, but follow their parents or carers. They are doing this either to seek reward or to avoid punishment. Through punishment and obedience (sub-stage 1), the child finds out about what is right and wrong through seeing the consequences of their actions. Individualism, instrumental purpose and exchange (sub-stage 2) results in the child learning that some actions and behaviours are rewarded. The child is also learning to avoid behaviours that might mean punishment. By the end of the pre-conventional stage the child is also beginning to enjoy helping people and has learned the 'If I help you, you might be able to help me' approach.

Kohlberg identified that, at first, children learn moral development through the behaviourist approach, i.e. desired behaviour being positively reinforced and unwanted behaviour being punished.

Conventional morality

The next stage of moral development consists of an awareness of group behaviour and the idea of what is and is not acceptable in society. The first sub-stage, often known as 'Good boy/nice girl', covers mutual interpersonal expectations, relationships and interpersonal conformity. Children come to believe that good behaviour pleases other people, e.g. parents, friends and teachers. They are also becoming aware of the motive factor, e.g. 'He didn't mean to drop it. He meant to help.'

The next sub-stage involves social systems and conscience, also referred to as law and order orientation (sub-stage 4). This is a widening out stage. Prior to this stage, children want to show good and correct behaviour to please people they know. At sub-stage 4 they become more aware of society's needs and interests, and what is deemed by society to be right or wrong. They are keen to obey regulations and laws.

Post-conventional or principled morality

This level is very different from the others. At this level, people do not accept the morality of a group or society unquestioningly. Demonstrators who break laws (e.g. animal-rights campaigners who illegally set animals free) would be demonstrating this level of morality. In the social contract sub-stage, rules and regulations are seen as useful tools to make sure that there is some protection and fairness in society. Those working at this level are prepared to tolerate rules being broken, if they see that those rules are unfair or unjust.

The final sub-stage, universal ethical principles, was in some ways an unclear one for Kohlberg and a difficult one to test. Those at this stage of morality development would be extremely principled people, not swayed by society and with inner morals that they have developed. Historically, people who may have reached this level are often killed or persecuted as they are seen as troublemakers unwilling to compromise their position.

Interview – Morality levels in a 7- and a 10-year-old

Q. 'Is it ever right to steal?'
A. 'No, you should never steal. Stealing is wrong. It's wrong to steal and it's bad.'
Q. 'Why is it wrong to steal?'
A. 'It's just wrong.'
(Responses from a 7-year-old)

Q. 'Is it ever right to steal?'
A. 'No. You should ask or earn money to buy things.'
Q. 'If someone had lots of things and was nasty and you had nothing, could you steal then?'
A. 'No. You might go to prison and then you would not be able to use anything that you had taken.'
(Responses from a 10-year-old)

Note how, in both sets of responses, although these children have learned that stealing is wrong, they are not considering the needs and feelings of the other person. In the 10-year-old's reasoning, thought is given to the consequences but not the nature of the action.

Social environment and moral development

Kohlberg makes it clear that cognitive development has a significant impact on moral development. Children and young people with good language skills, and those who have been given opportunities to reason and problem-solve, are more likely to be able to show high levels of moral reasoning. But this in itself is not enough. Children and young people also need to be in social situations that encourage discussion, explanation and exploration of moral issues. This has significant implications for the way in which we work with children. Rather than be told what is the 'right' answer, children need to be guided to higher levels of thinking by, for example, being asked questions and being given actual responsibilities for setting boundaries and deciding on consequences. Where this approach has been tried, it has been very successful in increasing young people's moral reasoning powers.

What does it mean in practice?

Bringing it all together

We have seen that moral development is quite complex. It involves cognitive development and language development but is also influenced by the social environment. Family, friends and settings such as school can all have an impact on moral development.

Children:

■ Remember that children's understanding of right and wrong is malleable and influenced by what they see, hear and experience.

■ Encourage discussion about rules, principles and right and wrong.

■ Do not expect that children will always be able to resist temptation.

■ Give positive feedback when children have tried to do the right thing.

■ Understand that children may say what is right and wrong, but there may be contradictions in their behaviour.

■ Be as consistent as possible in your own standards of behaviour and your expectations.

Young people:

■ Give young people opportunities for setting their own boundaries and rules.

■ Encourage discussion rather than simply 'telling' young people how they should behave.

■ Ask questions to promote higher levels of thinking, e.g. about intentions and consequences.

■ Encourage young people to explore issues that have particular meaning for them.

Pro-social development

Whilst moral development is about knowing right from wrong, pro-social development is about the way in which we help others. Examples of pro-social behaviour would include offering to hold a door open for someone or helping another person with their homework. Altruism is unselfish concern for others, which can lead to behaviours that risk the well-being of the person carrying out the behaviour. Altruism is often used in the context of pro-social behaviour, although it is usually seen as the extreme end of pro-social behaviour.

Are pro-social behaviours really selfish ones?

There is a school of thought that pro-social behaviours, such as helping someone carry a heavy box, and even altruistic behaviours, such as risking your life to save someone else's, are actually born out of self-interest. This is an intriguing proposal that is called 'universal egoism'. The idea is that by helping another person, there is some personal gain from the act. For example, stopping to help someone who has fallen over may make us feel good inside, whilst offering a friend a drink may result in being offered one at some time in the future.

So what about situations where someone puts their own life at risk to save another's? Here it is thought that, whilst the gain might not be personal, it might be about helping our species to survive. This could explain why many acts of altruism involve the saving of children and young people. Whether or not pro-social behaviours, including altruism, are really linked to self-interest will of course remain a matter of speculation. Such behaviours do however benefit our relationships with others and also contribute towards a cohesive society. This is why they are valued in children.

Development of pro-social behaviours in children

Even young children show pro-social behaviour. Many 2- and 3-year-olds will put an arm around another child to comfort them. As children get older, we may also see that they try to protect or advise others, especially children younger than themselves. Although such actions show some pro-social behaviour, children will mostly think about their own needs first rather than those of others. This type of thinking has been dubbed 'hedonistic reasoning' by researcher Nancy Einsberg.

From around 6 or 7 years of age hedonistic reasoning changes and children seem to be more aware of other's needs and begin to think about them. Einsberg calls this stage 'needs-orientated reasoning'. She also suggests that adolescents develop this type of thinking further and become aware not only of expectations in others, but also their own feelings when they do show pro-social behaviour. Having said this, the extent to which children think about others can vary dramatically. It can be a factor in determining whether children and young people find it easy to make and sustain relationships. It also relates to popularity, which was discussed earlier in the chapter (page 78).

Pro-social development from a behaviourist perspective

Behaviourists such as Albert Bandura take the line that pro-social development is closely linked to the behaviour of adults, i.e. it is learned. A child who has experienced being comforted by adults will be more likely to imitate this behaviour. Seeing what others do seems, therefore, important in helping children to learn to be helpful, although it appears that pro-social behaviours can also be strengthened by being acknowledged and the behaviour praised.

Helen Bee (2004) suggests that attributing pro-social behaviour to a child's characteristics helps the child develop an internal model of self-belief, e.g. 'I am a child who helps others.' Thus the child who helps another and is then told by an adult how kind they are, may well become more helpful. Helen Bee also suggests that children and young people benefit from being given responsibility and opportunities to demonstrate pro-social behaviour.

What does it mean in practice?

Developing pro-social behaviour

Think about the emotional environment that you are creating for children and young people.

■ Is it supportive, caring and warm?

■ Give clear guidelines on ways in which children and young people can be helpful, e.g. 'It would be helpful if you could share that toy.'

■ Create opportunities for children to take responsibility and be helpful, e.g. handing out paper or tidying away.

■ Explain the consequences of actions on others and talk about feelings.

■ Act as a role model by displaying thoughtful behaviour yourself.

Bullying and pro-social development

Earlier in this chapter we looked at bullying. We know that many onlookers will not necessarily intervene when another child is bullied. This may seem strange but the behaviour replicates itself in the adult world too. You have probably heard stories of people looking on without helping while someone is attacked or mugged, even in broad daylight and in crowded places. It would seem that some processes are taking place that either enable us to help others or cause us not to react.

Decision model

Research that looks at situations where onlookers have intervened shows that a decision-making process is taking place. One thing that seems to influence whether or not an onlooker will intervene is the number of other people who are around at the time. Ironically, people are less likely to help or intervene when there are others around. It would seem that, in such situations, feelings of responsibility towards the person needing help decrease. This may be explained by the way in which we check the reactions of others. If other onlookers also seem unsure or are not inclined to act, this may slow or prevent us from doing anything. Another factor is whether we know what to do or if we have the expertise to do it.

Arousal-cost-reward model

The 'arousal-cost-reward' model suggests that the decision to help or not may be linked to the benefits or cost to ourselves, assuming that we notice that someone needs our help in the first place. For example, people in a hurry may not stop to assist someone who is lost as stopping 'costs' them something: being late. The same person may behave differently on another day when they have plenty of time because there would be no 'cost'. Equally, another person may decide to stop and help because they know that they will feel guilty about not stopping afterwards. Feeling guilty is a 'cost', so by helping no 'cost' is incurred.

As well as evaluating cost, we may also be considering 'rewards' in our decisions to help or intervene. Helping may mean that recognition is given. This could be other people commenting about how thoughtful and kind we have been, or the person who has been helped may provide the recognition. We may also mentally 'reward' ourselves when we show pro-social behaviour and make ourselves feel good. With bullying, it may be that some children become aware that there could be a 'cost' to themselves if they intervene. They may reason that they may get hurt or become the next target, and so find it harder to intervene or get help.

▲ Why might this boy try to stop the fight?

Show your knowledge

1. What is meant by 'theory of mind' and how does it link to social development?

2. How does friendship group size change with age?

3. Give three characteristics of a 'popular' child.

4. How is moral development linked to cognitive development?

5. Why is it important for bullying to be taken as a serious issue by adults?

6. Explain what is meant by the 'no blame' approach to bullying.

Chapter 4

Cognitive development

Cognitive development is a significant area of development in children and young people and encompasses the skills needed to process and retain information, as well as the use of logic and thought. Whilst language and mathematical development can be seen as separate areas in young children, their roles are considered in this section alongside cognitive development as all three become increasingly intertwined.

This chapter is divided into the following sections:

- Brain development
- Piaget's and Vygotsky's theories of cognitive development
- Language and cognitive development
- Information processing skills and cognitive development
- Learning theories
- Intelligence
- Learning to read and write
- Learning mathematics

Brain development

A good starting point when looking at cognitive development is brain development. The study of how brains develop and function is a relatively new area of research and it is likely to have increasing relevance to the way in which we work with children and young people. It is becoming increasingly apparent that many cognitive functions (such as concentration, logic and memory) are linked to growth and development within the brain.

A quick guide to brain activity

Brain activity occurs when electrical pulses are sent between specialised cells in the brain. These cells, which are responsible for transmitting and receiving electrical signals, are known as neurons. It is useful to understand the basic structure of neurons and the way in which they connect with each other (see Figure 4.1).

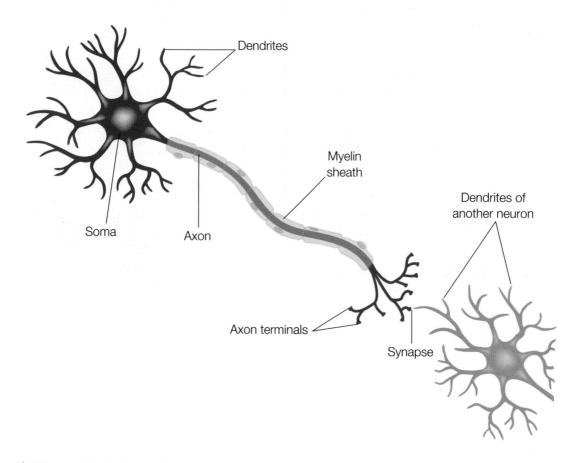

▲ **Figure 4.1** The basic structure of a neuron

Neurons have branch-like structures called dendrites that enable them to *receive* information. To *transmit* information, neurons have axons which end in a terminal. Electrical signals are sent between the axons of one neuron and the dendrites of another, although they do not actually touch each other. Instead there is a tiny gap between the axon and dendrites which is called a synapse. Chemicals called neurotransmitters are produced by neurons to bridge this gap (or synapse) to allow the electrical signal to pass to the next neuron.

Building connections

Neurons in themselves are ineffective. It is only when they work together to create pathways of connecting electrical pulses across the brain that things happen. For a simple action to take place, such as lifting an arm, millions of neurons will connect with each other and 'fire off' electrical signals virtually simultaneously. This means that the number of synapses and their complexity is all important when it comes to brain development.

Every new experience we have creates new connections of neurons within the brain, and repeated experiences create very strong and long-lasting connections. As well as making connections, the brain also loses connections through a process known as 'neural pruning'. Neural pruning is like a spring clean for the brain. Synapses that are no longer used or required are lost but, whilst this sounds destructive, it is actually quite positive in a developing brain. By stripping out redundant synapses, electrical pulses can move through the brain more effectively. In terms of a child's developing brain, neural pruning makes a significant difference, as we will see.

Did you know?

We are born with around 100 billion neurons.

The story so far...

Early brain development

Brain development begins well before birth. The majority of the 100 billion neurons that we have as adults are formed between the 10th and 20th week of pregnancy. In the final two months before birth, the dendrites and axons of the neurons develop. Neurons also begin the process of making connections, and those that have not made sufficiently strong connections are killed off. This is thought to be a reason why some children are born with learning disabilities.

At birth, whilst neurons are present, many areas of the brain are not yet activated. This is because, as well as neurons needing to make connections to create synapses, the axons of neurons need to be coated with a substance called myelin in order to work effectively. Myelin acts as an insulator and prevents electrical pulses from straying. The process of coating the axons is known as myelinisation and begins in the first few months of life, but is not completed until early adulthood.

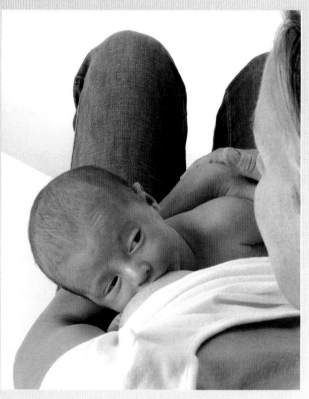

Alongside myelinisation, the first two years of life also see a threefold increase in the weight of the brain. This is as a result of the axons and dendrites increasing in size and an increasing number of synapses being made. Interestingly, the process of growth within the brain does not occur uniformly. Synapses made to enable visual processes are made earlier than those for language. It is not clear if synapse increase follows a pre-determined pattern, but the role of stimulation is definitely important.

At 18 months and thereafter, the brain prunes unused synapses. Babies who are stimulated and enjoy a rich environment of sensations and movement, but particularly exposure to language, should develop strong and dense synapses that will cope with pruning. On the other hand, babies

▲ The fat content in milk will help the myelinisation taking place in this baby's brain

who are deprived of stimulation and language may lose out, as pruning seems to take away those synapses that are not used and it is now clear that these cannot be replaced later.

Whilst much happens in terms of brain development in the first two years, things slow down afterwards, although new synapses continue to be made and the process of myelinisation continues. A further growth spurt occurs at around 4 years old which is linked to children's fluency in language and speech.

Brain development 6–16 years

Whilst significant amounts of growth take place in the first two years, further brain growth and development continues in a spurt-like fashion from 6 years of age right through until the end of adolescence.

Growth spurts

There are some significant growth spurts that result in astounding developmental progress during childhood and adolescence (see Figure 4.2).

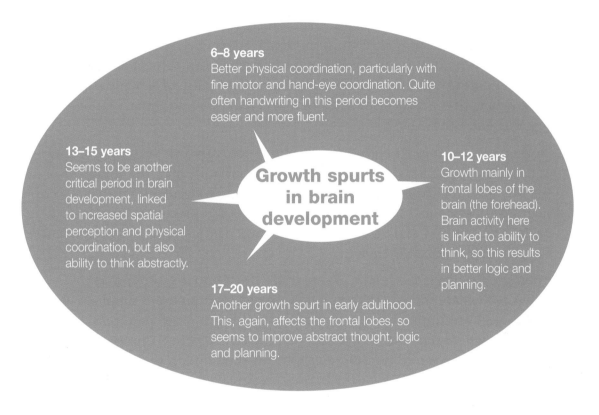

6–8 years
Better physical coordination, particularly with fine motor and hand-eye coordination. Quite often handwriting in this period becomes easier and more fluent.

13–15 years
Seems to be another critical period in brain development, linked to increased spatial perception and physical coordination, but also ability to think abstractly.

Growth spurts in brain development

10–12 years
Growth mainly in frontal lobes of the brain (the forehead). Brain activity here is linked to ability to think, so this results in better logic and planning.

17–20 years
Another growth spurt in early adulthood. This, again, affects the frontal lobes, so seems to improve abstract thought, logic and planning.

▲ **Figure 4.2** Growth spurts in brain development

Myelinisation

The process of coating the neurons with myelin also plays an important part in cognitive and physical functions. The myelinisation of neurons affecting gross motor movements finishes at about 6 years. This is why children of this age start to run faster and are also able to hop and skip. In terms of cognitive function, myelinisation seems to play a part in the speed at which information can be processed and analysed. Whilst the process has begun in the first 6 years of life, it isn't completed until around 12 years of age. This would account for the differences in the speed at which children can, for example, play games such as 'snap'. Younger children can realise that a match has been made, but older children are quicker to realise and then shout out.

As well as speed of information processing, myelinisation also seems to be responsible for improvements in concentration. Throughout the 6–16 years period, myelinisation means that longer attention spans are possible and, with this, the ability to decide what needs to be focused on.

Can fish oils improve concentration?

There is some evidence to suggest that diet makes a difference to brain function and development. Whilst most researchers believe that diet during pregnancy can affect brain development in the unborn baby, it is also thought that diet during childhood can also play a part. In particular, some studies have shown that a fatty acid called omega-3 may have an impact on children's learning and behaviour.

Omega-3 is found in a range of foods, but particularly fish such as mackerel and herring. It is thought that omega-3 is crucial in healthy development of the brain as it is involved in the efficient transfer of electrical pulses between neurons. It is claimed that many children's diets do not contain the correct balance of omega-3 and omega-6 (another fatty acid), and that this imbalance can affect the brain's efficiency.

Interestingly, when the results of one study (the Durham study) were published, where school children had been given an omega-3 supplement with significant improvements in reading, spelling and behaviour observed, a major chemist sold out of omega-3 supplements within 24 hours! Whilst parents may be keen to try out omega-3 with their children, some scientists are more sceptical, claiming that the brain is extremely complex and that the trials carried out so far, whilst interesting, are not yet conclusive.

Research it!

Look into both sides of the omega-3 debate by using a search engine on the internet or by visiting websites that explore this issue. A link to one such website has been made available at www.heinemann.co.uk/hotlinks. Enter the express code 983XP to access the links.

Next time you go to a supermarket, keep an eye out for products, including milk, where omega-3 has been added.

Piaget's and Vygotsky's theories of cognitive development

The work of Jean Piaget (1896–1980) and Lev Vygotsky (1896–1934) have had a major influence on the way in which educationalists and others have considered children's cognitive development. Piaget's work has also acted as a foundation for further theories and research. Using detailed observations and without the benefit of today's brain scanners, Piaget was uncannily accurate in some of his predictions and thoughts about cognitive development in light of what we now know about the brain.

Piaget's approach to cognitive development

Piaget's approach to cognitive development is sometimes known as 'constructivist'. This is because he identified that children were active rather than passive in learning. At the time of his work, this was a revolutionary concept as there was a pervading view that children needed to be taught, shown or praised in order to learn. However, Piaget believed that children 'constructed' their own theories and logic about what was happening around and to them. Piaget felt that there was a process at work by which children were able to think and develop ideas and then adapt and refine them where necessary.

Piaget used the term 'schema' to mean the basis of an idea, a thought or even a sequence of physical movements. An example of a physical schema would be the way that a baby playfully drops a spoon from a highchair. The baby has learned a 'drop' schema and is likely from this point to drop other items and watch them fall. As the child repeatedly drops items, the idea about objects falling is being developed and the schema strengthened. Piaget called the taking in of new information 'assimilation'.

But what would happen if one day the baby dropped something and it bounced back? This would not correlate with what had happened to the other things that were dropped. This becomes another stage in Piaget's process that he called 'accommodation'. Piaget argued that children had the capacity to refine and adapt initial schemas to 'accommodate' new knowledge or experiences. In turn, the adapted schemas are tried out to see if they work.

▲ Every time something is dropped, the schema is reinforced

In our example, the baby may spend time looking closely at objects before dropping them. He may at first think that bouncing occurs only when objects are passed to him, but then has to adapt the schema once more when this does not hold true. Finally, he starts looking at the objects and recognises that balls bounce but spoons do not. Piaget called the reconciling of the new information with the widening and refinement of the child's schemas 'equilibration' – as if everything now balances.

Piaget also identified that there are three points in childhood when radical overhauls of schemas take place. These three points of equilibration form the basis of Piaget's four stages of cognitive development, as each time a radical overhaul took place, the child was able to make a huge cognitive shift and move on to the next stage.

Piaget also felt that both nature and nurture are at work in terms of cognitive development. Experiences and interactions with adults and others will play a part in what the child assimilates, whilst the processes of adapting schemas and equilibration are inborn. Piaget assumed that brain maturation is a process and used this to account for differences in rates of development between similarly aged children.

Concrete operations (6–11 years)

The next stage that Piaget identified in cognitive development he labelled 'concrete operations'. The term 'operations' was used to describe a range of more abstract and mental schemas, such as the ability to use addition and subtraction. In this period, children master several principles that Piaget thought of as critical for logic.

Reversibility

Reversibility is the ability to understand that many mental and physical actions are reversible. In terms of mathematical understanding it is crucial, for example, that children understand that $1 + 4 = 5$, but equally that $4 + 1$ also makes 5. With younger children, reversibility is a problem and it shows itself if you pour a quantity of coloured water into a tall thin container and then pour it into a wider but shorter one. Children will often say that some of the liquid has disappeared. Acquiring an understanding of reversibility also means that children can begin to use simple logic and apply information that they have gained from one situation to another (although they will do better in situations where they can handle objects or have previous experience and knowledge). The term 'concrete operations' is therefore a reflection of the idea that children need to see, experience or physically handle things.

Class inclusion

Children during this stage also become more skilled at understanding how things relate to each other, known as 'class inclusion'. For example, they can understand that their mother is also their grandmother's daughter, whilst also being their aunt's sister. Pre-operational children tend to find this conceptually difficult. The progress that children make in the period of concrete operations is not uniform, as many teachers in primary schools will know. Children may be able to work out that 45 + 15 = 60 and that 60 – 15 = 45, but may not be sure how to look for their PE kit if they cannot immediately see it.

Formal operations (12–16 years)

Piaget's final stage is that of 'formal operations', which Piaget suggested occurred between the ages of 12–16 for most young people. Piaget was clear that the move from concrete operations to formal operations is not automatic and that, because of the inherited aspect of cognitive development, not all young people will even attain formal operations. The term 'formal operations' relates to a level of more abstract thinking that is not dependent on having prior knowledge or experience. There are several skills connected to this stage.

Systematic problem-solving

Systematic problem-solving is about our ability to think rationally and systematically through a problem rather than simply guessing or using trial and error. For example, does a young person when faced with a combination lock try out random numbers or go through number combinations systematically? When you find that an electrical appliance does not work, do you work through the probable causes one by one or do you sometimes use trial and error?

> **Did you know?**
>
> Researchers looking at Piaget's theory have noticed that even when adults are capable of using formal operations, they may still at times use the skills associated with concrete operations

Hypothetico–deductive reasoning

This is the way in which we use logic in situations that we have no experience of, hence 'hypothetico' standing for hypothetical. Deductive reasoning, as it is also known, is the ability to use information to extrapolate other information, as in the following example:

A boy who is critically ill is taken to hospital by his father. The doctor enters the examination room to see the patient, takes one look at the boy and cries, 'Oh my son, my son!' Explain the relationship between the boy and the doctor. (The answer is that the doctor is the boy's mother.)

Whilst children in the concrete operations stage are using logic, they tend to find it hard to make predictions about things of which they have no experience. In the formal operations stage, young people are increasingly able to speculate and make rational decisions accordingly. This shows itself not only in the type of mathematical questions that they can answer, but also in the way in which they are able to consider questions such as 'What would be the benefits of taxing foods that are high in fats?'

Naïve realism

As part of the formal operations stage, Piaget felt that young people's ability to question, imagine and speculate can make them aware of shortcomings in society. They now have the cognitive sophistication to construct an ideal society (e.g. a peaceful society) and, with this in mind, are able to reflect on the nature of the society in which they live. This can be positive as some young people are then driven to look for ways of making society fairer and closer to the society that they can imagine. Naïve realism also means that some young people become aware of what they perceive as hypocrisy amongst adults, such as teachers who in health promotion lessons talk about the dangers of smoking, but who smoke themselves!

Observing theory

Observe children and young people of different ages carrying out the same task. The task can be anything that is practical but also requires some logical thought. A good example might be to set the task of preparing some bubble mixture on the basis that, once it has been made, some more mixture must be made that is exactly the same. This would require washing-up liquid, water and, as an optional extra, liquid glycerine, plus containers, pens and paper.

- Watch to see how each child or young person approaches the task.

- Can they recreate exactly the same mixture twice?

Criticisms of Piaget's theory

It is worth being aware of some difficulties with Piaget's theory that subsequent research has produced. Firstly, there is research that shows that Piaget may have underestimated the capabilities of children in some cognitive tasks, particularly in his descriptions of the development of babies and young children. For example, babies have better memories than Piaget suggested and young children can imagine what someone else is thinking.

There is also some criticism of the 'stage-like' development that Piaget describes. Some researchers believe cognitive development to be more continuous, not following a step-by-step process. This being said, there is no doubt that Piaget's work has stood the test of time in many respects and that his basic observations of development, particularly for older children and young adults, seem to be fairly accurate and have even stood up to cross-cultural research.

Vygotsky's approach to cognitive development

In recent years, Vygotsky's work has also been influencing practice with children and young people. Vygotsky is well-known for believing that cognitive development is very much reliant on the input of others. His theory is underpinned by the notion that learning is a social process. Whilst Piaget suggested that adults are important in providing developmental opportunities for children, Vygotsky believed that adults are crucial in extending cognitive development through a guiding and teaching role.

Vygotsky suggested that adults could take children to a higher level of cognition through their interactions with them. Vygotsky's theory therefore emphasises the importance of language in learning. To explain how this process takes place, Vygotsky used the term 'Zone of Proximal Development', shortened to ZPD. The idea is that children may reach a

▲ Vygotsky believed that interaction with adults can greatly improve a child's cognitive development

certain level of intellectual competence, but without an adult they may not be able to extend it further, even though they have the underlying capacity. Vygotsky's theory is interesting as there is plenty of evidence that children who have not had access to quality interactions and language have lower IQ scores than those who have. Whilst Vygotsky believed in parents, teachers and other adults guiding children, it is essential to stress the interactive view that he had of learning and also the importance of the relationship between the adult and child.

What does it mean in practice?

Applying Vygotsky's theories

- **Relationships are key to learning** This is demonstrated by the way in which children and young people do well with adults that they respect and enjoy being with.

- **Language is a major tool for learning** Adults need to talk to children and young people so that they can develop ideas and use language to think. This does not mean talking 'at' children and young people!

- **Adults can help children and young people develop their potential** Vygotsky's theory is that children and young people can develop further from the point at which we may be working with them. This means that observation is important, but only in working out what the next steps are and our role in building on children's and young people's current levels.

Language and cognitive development

Both Piaget and Vygotsky were clear that language was an important ingredient in the development of learning and thinking. The key to understanding the role of language in cognitive development is to imagine a situation where you could only talk about whatever was in front of you at the time. This would be extremely restricting as you would not be able to talk about past events, the future, feelings and, of course, ideas and concepts. Language is therefore essential in order to think in the abstract.

The story so far...

Early language development

Language learning begins before birth when the unborn child is already hearing and beginning to recognise tunes and the tone of its mother's voice. Both nature and nurture are clearly at work.

▲ Even before birth, a child will be learning about language by hearing its mother's voice

The ability to learn language is common to all humans, but babies and young children need the interaction of adults and other children for this learning to take place. Research shows that quality interaction in the first year of life plays an essential role in later cognitive development, as it encourages language learning. The first year or so of a baby's life is spent learning the skills of communication, such as eye contact, pitch and tone of voice, and gaining the understanding of a few key words. This phase is known as the pre-linguistic phase as babies are not using words, although they will be trying to communicate by crying, babbling and, later, pointing.

At around 13 months, most babies begin to use sounds with consistent meaning, e.g. 'dada' meaning dad or parent. For the next few months, the number of words acquired slowly increases, but this changes once children reach the end of their second year. At this point, children's vocabulary increases at a significant rate and they begin to put two words together to make simple sentences. From this point onwards, language really begins to develop, with children going on to use plurals, questions and beginning to understand grammatical rules. By the age of 3, an adult unfamiliar with the child should be able to understand what they are saying. By 4 years old, most children should be reasonably fluent, although odd grammatical errors and speech immaturity will continue until around 7 years of age.

Using language for organising and self-directing

As well as language opening up the ability for abstract thinking, language also helps us to organise ourselves practically. At first, this use of language is external and we will see that young children often think aloud (much to the irritation of many adults!). From around 6 or 7 years, thinking aloud becomes less of an occurrence as children learn to think 'inside' their head.

The ability to use language to direct and organise has a huge impact on children's and young people's behaviour. They may refrain from grabbing something because an 'internal voice' reasons with them. In the same way, they may take time to think about what needs to be put into their school bag. The importance of language in relation to thinking and behaviour means that children or young people who do not have good language skills are disadvantaged. They may present more behavioural problems and may find it hard to organise themselves.

Observing theory

Observe the way in which children and young people use speech in order to organise their thoughts. Whilst it is relatively easy to observe in young children, as they often talk to themselves as they play, it can be harder to see in older children and young people. In order to watch this, give older children and young people some cards with numbers on them. Ask them to add them up as quickly as possible in their heads. Watch to see if you can 'hear' them think!

Information processing skills and cognitive development

An area of research which complements Piaget's and Vygotsky's approaches is information processing. This looks at what happens to information that the brain receives: how we store it, use it and sometimes lose it.

Concentration

Concentration is a skill necessary to process and retain information. Concentration requires sustained attention on a particular focus. In order to achieve this, some level of arousal is necessary to gain attention in the first place. Babies and young children can concentrate, but not to the same extent as older children and young people. This is partly because concentration is an active skill that requires us to consciously ignore irrelevant information that we are receiving, otherwise we become distracted. This means that, whilst a baby may stare at a mobile, it will stop once it hears the sound of a door opening or if it is shown another toy.

By the age of about 14, most young people have mastered the skills of concentration, although variables such as tiredness, hunger and interest need to be taken into account. One group of children and young people for whom concentration is difficult are those with Attention Deficit Hyperactivity Disorder (generally known as ADHD) where their arousal levels are set too low. This means that the amount of stimuli needed for them to focus their attention is greater than for other children of the same age. This results in difficulty concentrating or sitting still in situations where the stimuli are not sufficient to hold their attention.

Memory

A major part of information processing is the use of memory: learning cannot take place without memory! Memory, and how it functions, is an ongoing area of research, but it seems that a system is in place that gives us a short-term or 'working' memory and a long-term memory (see Figure 4.3). The starting point for laying down any type of memory at all is the receiving of information through our senses. This information then goes through a filtering process that is referred to as a sensory buffer. At this point, much of the information that we receive can be lost, either because it is irrelevant or because it has not made much impact.

From the sensory buffer, information is then registered in the short-term memory or 'working' memory. The short-term memory has a very limited time span and capacity. It is thought that the short-term memory, on average, only holds seven items of information at any time. This is why a stream of numbers (e.g. 7, 3, 1, 8, 2, 6, 5, 9, 4, 5, 1, etc.) will quickly be forgotten unless a strategy is used for holding on to it. From the short-term memory, information is transferred to the long-term memory, although this is also a two-way process, i.e. information already stored in the long-term memory helps us make sense of new information in the short-term memory. Thus if we are trying to learn a new word in another language, associations between its sound and a similar word we already know might be made, helping us to remember it.

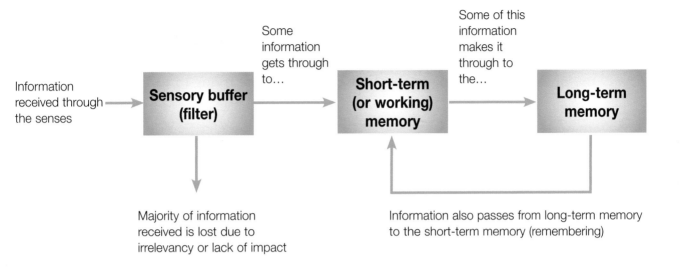

Information received through the senses → **Sensory buffer (filter)**

Some information gets through to... → **Short-term (or working) memory**

Some of this information makes it through to the... → **Long-term memory**

Majority of information received is lost due to irrelevancy or lack of impact

Information also passes from long-term memory to the short-term memory (remembering)

▲ **Figure 4.3** The structure of memory

Memory strategies

Possessing a range of memory strategies allows older children and young people to retain more information as it travels through the sensory buffer and into the short-term memory. Memory strategies are not available in the same way to young children and this may explain why they need frequent reminders. Some of the following memory strategies you will be probably be familiar with.

Rehearsal

Rehearsal is a strategy whereby information is repeated. For example, a telephone number that you need to remember may be muttered under your breath several times.

Clustering

We have seen that the short-term memory's capacity is extremely limited. To make more of its capacity for seven or so pieces of information, information can be grouped together. Instead of seeing a phone number as 0, 1, 3, 2, 6, 4, 3, 5, 7, 7, 8 (which is eleven pieces of information), it can instead be remembered as 01326 435 778, which is now just three pieces of information. Clustering can also be used to group information by putting it into categories. A list of words may be better remembered by, for example, grouping all the words that are names of animals together, or grouping all the words that start with the same letter together. Combining clustering with rehearsal creates a very powerful way of boosting the amount of information that can be remembered.

Elaboration

Elaboration is a sophisticated strategy that involves looking for ways of making information more relevant. To remember a person's name, you might think about what they are wearing, e.g. 'Barry of the blue jacket'. Elaboration is a useful strategy for young people to use when they are trying to revise.

Retrieval of information

As well as finding ways of storing information, it is also important to have ways of searching your memory in order to retrieve information stored there. For example, someone may ask you the name of a road that you should know, but you struggle to remember the name immediately. You have been unsuccessful in retrieving this information from your memory.

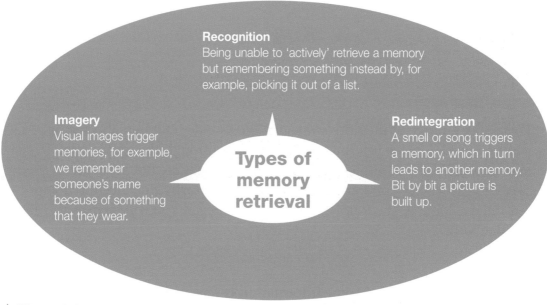

Recognition
Being unable to 'actively' retrieve a memory but remembering something instead by, for example, picking it out of a list.

Imagery
Visual images trigger memories, for example, we remember someone's name because of something that they wear.

Types of memory retrieval

Redintegration
A smell or song triggers a memory, which in turn leads to another memory. Bit by bit a picture is built up.

▲ **Figure 4.4**

Metacognition

Metacognition is the ability to be consciously aware of your thinking processes. A good example is the way that we might think to ourselves, 'That's interesting. I didn't know that before.' By doing this, we are consciously recognising the boundaries of our knowledge.

Metacognition skills are vital in information processing and, therefore, overall cognitive development. As with other areas of development, metacognition skills develop over time. Some researchers believe that it is superior metacognition skills that account for the differences between children's academic achievements, although there is also the view that this might be due to inherited differences.

Metamemory

Metamemory refers to knowing how to use your memory efficiently in terms of storing information that you want to keep and retrieving information that is available. Being able to have some control over your memory processes means that you can be active in deciding what you would like to remember and have strategies to recall stored information. This is extremely helpful in many everyday situations, such as learning someone's phone number, but is significant in terms of achievement in schools where children's and young people's qualifications may depend on their ability to revise and then recall information in an exam.

Other skills of metamemory include the ability to scan your memory to help you retrieve information. This requires active and conscious use of your mind and again is something that becomes available with development.

The story so far...
Information processing in young children

It is thought that it is not until 4–5 years old that children are aware that they are thinking and that others are thinking too. Young children also compartmentalise information and do not necessarily connect it to what they already know or consider how it might be relevant in solving problems. Young children clearly have memories, although they may not be able to manipulate them easily. This is why 3-year-olds will find it hard on the way home to remember what they were doing at nursery that morning and will often say they did 'nothing'!

Information processing 6–11 years

It is in this period that children's information processing skills show a marked improvement, particularly at the latter end of this period. Metacognition skills are beginning to develop, with most 7- and 8-year-olds recognising that they think and that others are thinking too. Advances in metacognition skills means that, by the end of this period, many children recognise that they may need to concentrate a little bit more at times and are better at consciously maintaining attention.

There is also a significant shift in terms of memory and using metamemory skills. Again this increases with children's age. An example is the way in which children over 6 begin to use rehearsal strategies to help memorise information, but older children will rehearse more efficiently by grouping or clustering information. During this period, children also start to be able to search their memories, although this is clearly a developing skill and adults may need to provide prompts to help children do this.

Chapter 4 Cognitive development

Information processing 12–16 years

A further shift takes place in information processing in this period although, again, speed and efficiency increase over time. Interestingly, individual differences can still be seen, with some 12-year-olds able to process information as effectively as some 15-year-olds. Some of the gains in speed of information processing are likely to be a result of young people simply 'knowing' and being able to retrieve information quickly from their long-term memories, rather than needing to consciously work out a problem. A good example of this is retrieving mathematical number facts. A 4-year-old may still be working out that $4 - 1 = 3$, whilst this is simply 'known' by a young person.

'Knowing', in this context, is referred to as automaticity and allows you to focus the rest of your mental effort where it is needed. Information that is recalled in this way tends to have been practised. Young people also have advantages in terms of information processing as they have had more experiences than younger children. This means that, in theory, they should be able to make more connections between different pieces of information that they have stored. Young people can therefore use the elaboration memory strategy, although as a metacognition skill they must consciously choose to use it. Metamemory keeps on improving, with young people able to consciously use the type of retrieval strategies that we have looked at earlier in this section.

What does it mean in practice?

Is learning by rote useful?

Over the years, there have been many approaches to teaching children mathematics and reading. Learning by rote (memorising something purely by repeating it) used to be a popular way before the advent of Piaget's theory. Children would often chant their multiplication tables or the capitals of the world in order to learn them.

We can see from looking at the different memory strategies that rehearsing would enable children to 'remember' information and that a certain level of automaticity might be achieved. Whilst this might seem positive, it is also important to recognise that learning by rote alone does not ensure conceptual understanding. Thus whilst learning multiplication tables or key words for reading is important, it is essential that opportunities are given for putting the learning into context.

- What do you know as a result of rote learning?

- How did you learn your multiplication tables?

Consider how the increase in children's information processing skills links to brain development and also Piaget's cognitive development theory.

Learning theories

Whilst cognitive development theories look at the processes of understanding and use of logic, there are also theories that consider *how* we learn. These are called 'learning theories' and are useful in understanding behaviour, but also in providing practical advice about how we might encourage children and young people to learn. The two learning theories that we are going to explore focus primarily on the environment (i.e. what happens to children and young people), and so take a nurture perspective.

1. Operant conditioning
2. Social cognitive learning

Operant conditioning

We have already touched upon Skinner's operant conditioning theory in Chapter 3 Social development (see page 93), but the theory also lends itself to cognitive development, and it has been very influential in this area. Elements of operant conditioning can be seen in practice not only in schools, but also in shops (reward points).

In the simplest of terms, the theory suggests that we are likely to repeat behaviours that have been reinforced. A baby might, by accident, drop a spoon on to the floor, but then want to repeat the action because the spoon made an interesting sound. The sound of the spoon has acted as a reinforcer.

▲ Skinner experimented with rats, who were rewarded with food every time they pressed on a pedal – a form of operant conditioning

Reinforcers that encourage repetition of a behaviour can be divided into two kinds:

1. positive reinforcers
2. negative reinforcers.

Positive reinforcers are likely to make us repeat behaviour where we get something we desire. For example, children are very likely to repeat a behaviour if they gain attention, praise or rewards (e.g. sweets or stickers). Negative reinforcers are likely to make us repeat behaviour as well, but this is in order to bring a situation that is disliked to an end. For example, a parent whose son has been on the phone for too long might threaten him with disconnecting it if the call does not come to an end. The son says a rapid goodbye and ends the conversation. Negative reinforcement was used by the parent in order to encourage their son not to spend too long on the phone. The parent will probably find that they are less likely to use the same threat in the future.

Which type of reinforcements work best?

Skinner suggested that using positive reinforcement was the most effective way of encouraging new learning and of shaping behaviour. This is why schools and parenting classes encourage a positive style of working on children's behaviour.

It is also worth remembering that it is not possible to know what is acting as a reinforcer until we see that a behaviour is repeated. For example, if we look again at the example of the baby dropping a spoon on the floor, if the spoon fell but the baby was deaf, the sound would not act as reinforcement. There would be something else acting as positive reinforcement. This has implications for reward schemes or finding ways of motivating children and young people. Sometimes it is assumed that all children and young people will enjoy and respond to the same things. This, of course, is not true and so, whilst a system of collecting commendations (stars, certificates, etc.) might have a positive effect on some children, it may make little difference to others.

Unexpected positive reinforcers

As adults, it is worth considering in some situations what positive reinforcers might be at work when children's or young people's behaviour is inappropriate. A common mistake is for adults, when they are providing a punishment, a deterrent or trying to prevent a behaviour, to be unaware that they are actually encouraging a behaviour, simply by giving the child attention for the behaviour. For example, a young person calling out in class may be asked by the teacher to be quiet. However, the young person continues to call out, despite the fact that the teacher feels the behaviour has been punished. On the contrary, drawing attention to the calling out may have acted as a positive reinforcer, with the young person pleased to get the attention of not just the teacher, but the rest of the class. Not responding, but ensuring the pace of the lesson picked-up, might have proved more successful. When in the company of children and young people, observing and considering what is working and, more importantly, what is not proving effective is therefore essential.

Primary and secondary reinforcers

There are some reinforcers that give us instant pleasure, satisfaction or meet a need. These are referred to as primary reinforcers. Chocolate is a primary reinforcer because most people find that, once they put it into their mouths, they enjoy the taste.

Secondary reinforcers are different because they, in themselves, do not give us satisfaction, but we learn that they symbolise primary reinforcement. A good example of secondary reinforcement in our daily lives is money. Coins and notes do not give us reward, but we learn that they can be used to buy something that will give us primary reinforcement, for example, food. Supermarkets and other retailers use secondary reinforcers to make us loyal shoppers. Reward cards work on the principle that you gain points when you purchase items in a particular chain of store. When you have sufficient points, you can then trade them for something that you want.

As children become older, there is a tendency for adults to use more secondary reinforcers with them. Older children and young people may be given pocket money if they have done tasks around the home. In this example, the money is acting as a secondary reinforcer. Secondary reinforcers can work well and help behaviour to change over a longer period of time, but it is important that they are used only with children and young people who are able to understand delayed gratification. Some children and young people may respond better to being given a primary reinforcer at the time, as we will see in the next paragraph.

Timing of reinforcements

The timing of a reinforcement does seem to be critical. A reinforcement that is close to the action or behaviour is more powerful than one that is delayed. Giving a smile or encouragement during an activity will be more powerful than waiting until the end of the day to give it. Interestingly, many undesired behaviours, such as rocking on chairs, running in corridors or chewing gum, are all reinforced 'at the time'. They are also primary reinforcers as they are pleasurable. The combination of a primary reinforcer and the immediacy of timing of the reinforcement makes a strong reinforcer.

Timing of reinforcements also has implications for when children and young people do homework. A positive comment on a piece of homework that is returned rapidly will have more effect than one that is returned after a few weeks.

Schedules of reinforcement

It might be assumed that a reinforcement is needed every time an action takes place. Surprisingly, this is not the case. Skinner found that partial or intermittent reinforcements tend to lead to more persistent behaviours. A gambler does not need to win every time in order to keep playing. The nature of 'sometimes' and random reinforcements is well expressed by a 14-year-old boy:

'When my mum goes shopping, I always nag her to get me a bar of chocolate. It doesn't work every time, but it's still worth trying it on.'

(Harry)

The unconscious nature of learning

Whilst some learning is definitely conscious and we are aware of the reinforcers, this is not true all of the time. We may not, for example, consciously associate our loyalty to a supermarket with their reward point scheme. Some learning is situation-specific and, once in the situation, we behave in a certain way because our behaviour has been reinforced in the same situation before. We may not even be conscious of our actions. A smoker trying to give up may accept a cigarette from a friend who smokes without making a conscious decision; it is just what they are used to doing. Understanding that our responses are often linked to previous experiences of being in the same situation is important.

The unconscious nature of learning has practical implications. If behaviour has been repeatedly reinforced in the past and needs to be changed, one option is to change the situation so that the usual behaviour does not 'fit'. For example, a 'difficult' and whingey baby may not be so difficult when handled by someone new to them. This is probably because the responses to the behaviour by the new person will be different and so will not reinforce the behaviour. The term 'honeymoon period' is often used by adults when they first work with and produce positive changes in the behaviour of children or young people who have a track record of difficult behaviour.

What does it mean in practice?

Using operant conditioning

There are many practical applications of the operant conditioning theory for those working with children and young people. Several seem like common sense, but they can often be neglected in practice!

- **Positive interactions are vital** Children and young people are more likely to learn and show appropriate behaviour if they have positive interactions with adults.
- **Activities, lessons and situations must be enjoyable** This might seem obvious but it is absolutely crucial, especially when children and young people are doing something new. Enjoyment acts as a positive reinforcer.
- **Demonstrating success** Children will repeat an activity or work harder when they have had some success or can see that they will be successful. Achieving something, or seeing that achievement is within reach, is a positive reinforcer.
- **The need for acknowledgement and encouragement** We all benefit from being acknowledged and encouraged. Children and young people are no different. Attention is a positive reinforcer provided it is done sensitively. However, it is worth remembering that some children and young people prefer not to be praised in front of classmates, but may appreciate written comments or a quiet word.
- **Provision of feedback** Feedback is also important as it helps children and young people know how to get further reinforcements in the future. Statements such as 'Good boy' do not give much information to a child, whereas 'Well done! You remembered to put the toys away' tells the child that putting toys away was the good behaviour.
- **Timing of reinforcements** When trying to change behaviour, remember that delaying a reinforcement will lessen its effectiveness. This means a smile or a word of encouragement during an activity may have more of an effect than waiting until the end of a session.
- **Achievable secondary reinforcers** Secondary reinforcers, such as star charts and commendations, can work well with some children and young people but they must be achievable. A good analogy is the realisation that you have to make 2,000 trips to a supermarket to get a discount of 5 pence!
- **Change the script** New situations create perfect opportunities for adults and children to change reinforcement patterns. As adults, we too are reinforced as we deal with behaviour. This can create cycles of behaviour and responses in both adults and children. Changing a situation by changing our usual responses, adjusting the environment or planning new activities can be highly effective. This is why children and young people are often so well behaved on outings, as both they and the adults are put into new situations and the usual responses do not 'fit'.
- **Review the effects of reinforcements** Reinforcements are only reinforcements if they actually change behaviour. As children and young people are all unique individuals, it may be that one strategy may work for one but not for another. There should also be evidence of a change in behaviour. Thus it is important to observe carefully and reflect on what is happening. More than one reinforcement might be at work, or one might be having more effect. For example, a young person offered more pocket money by her parents for revising may find that chatting with friends on the internet is a more powerful reinforcer. Although more pocket money would seem to be a good incentive to study, it is a secondary reinforcer competing with a primary reinforcer (chatting on the internet, which offers instant pleasure).
- **Positive reinforcers are more effective in the long term** Skinner's research clearly showed that positive reinforcers influence learning in the longer term. Threats or punishments may have some short-term influence, but they do not make a difference in the longer term.

Social cognitive learning

This theory looks at the way in which children and young people learn through observing and then imitating in a process called 'modelling'. This is an interesting theory that has been developed over time, principally by Albert Bandura. Originally Bandura called this theory the 'social learning theory', but he has since considered the cognitive elements involved in it. As with the operant conditioning theory, there are no developmental stages but, by considering the cognitive elements, Bandura has attempted to explain why some actions are learned whilst others are not.

Learning through modelling

In the 1960s, Bandura was able to show through a classic experiment that children would perform actions that they had previously seen an adult do. The experiment involved showing children a film of an adult with a large inflatable doll known as a 'Bobo doll'. Three groups of children watched a different version of the film: one with the adult hitting the doll with another adult intervening and punishing them, one with the adult hitting the doll and another adult ignoring their behaviour and one film with the adult hitting the doll and being encouraged by another adult. Afterwards, the groups of children were put in a room with the Bobo doll and their responses observed. The children who had seen the adult's aggressive behaviour being either ignored or encouraged by the other adult, replicated the adult's actions. The group of children who had seen the adult being punished by the other adult showed little aggressive behaviour towards the Bobo doll. The overwhelming conclusion drawn from this classic experiment was that the children were influenced by the adults' actions.

Cognitive elements

Bandura explored what type of cognitive elements are required for social cognitive learning to take place. He identified four cognitive elements.

1. **Attention** Firstly, children and young people need to be interested enough to pay attention and to notice what the adult or other child is doing. In addition, they have to focus on the right elements and avoid distractions or the irrelevant. For example, an adult might stop and blow their nose whilst logging onto a computer, but the nose blow is irrelevant to the process of logging onto the computer. As we have seen earlier, being able to filter out the irrelevant and focus attention is a skill that develops over time.

2. **Encoding and retrieving information** In order to learn, information has to be encoded into the long-term memory in order to be retrieved. As memory use becomes more sophisticated with age, some information might not get stored. This is likely to be information that requires higher levels of processing where it is important to understand meaning. Copying actions of others is usually easier as this information is encoded visually and we might see 'pictures' in our memories of what we have seen.

3. **Opportunity to reproduce actions** Children and young people also need to be in the position where they can replicate what they have seen, e.g. an 8-year-old cannot play around and light a match if no matches are available. A sufficient level of physical skills might also be necessary, e.g. an 8-year-old needs a certain level of fine motor skills in order to use the matches.

4. **Motivation** Reason and motivation are other ingredients. Children and young people might find the action itself interesting or there may be a desire to 'become' the person that they have watched. They may also have seen that a reinforcement, such as admiration of others, is a result of the action. For example, a 7-year-old may notice in an after-school club that other children laugh at a boy who makes silly sounds and so will be motivated to try this out.

The role of reinforcements

Social cognitive theory and operant conditioning are not necessarily competing theories and can work hand in hand. A child might learn something through modelling and then have a reinforcement. For example, a 10-year-old might watch how a football player shuffles his feet to confuse his opponent before kicking the ball and scoring a goal. The child may then try out the behaviour himself. If a goal is scored, this footwork is likely to become a feature of the child's play. In addition to accepting the role of external reinforcements, Bandura also believes that another category of reinforcements is used, known as intrinsic reinforcements.

Intrinsic reinforcements

Intrinsic reinforcements do not come from other people, but are what we feel inside. If we feel good about what we have just done, we are more likely to repeat the action. A child might try to ride a bicycle because her sister can do it (modelling), but may also enjoy the satisfaction and challenge of learning a new skill (intrinsic reinforcement). Intrinsic reinforcements are perhaps the best reinforcements, as external reinforcements such as certificates or praise are not always available. Intrinsic reinforcements mean that the child in our example may want to practise riding a bike more for themselves than for the approval of adults.

What does it mean in practice?

Using social cognitive learning

This theory, whilst easy to understand, has many implications for adults working with children and young people.

- **Role models** The theory implies that we are all potential role models. Children and young people will observe the way that we talk, smile and use hand gestures, as well as those things we want them to copy (and those we do not, such as smoking or swearing).

- **Intrinsic reinforcements** A criticism of traditional external reinforcements (e.g. stickers, certificates and even praise) is the possibility that learning is dependent only on adult approval. Talking to children and young people about how they feel and encouraging them to recognise good feelings themselves is therefore thought to be a good strategy to promote independence.

- **Using 'show' as a way of teaching** As children and young people learn from observing, modelling can prove to be highly effective as a teaching strategy. Attitudes and interests are often copied. For example, parents who play musical instruments are more likely to have children interested in music. We can capitalise on this by doing ourselves what we would like children and young people to learn. Painting alongside young people or writing alongside primary children are effective ways of assisting learning.

▲ The behaviour of young people can be influenced by the behaviour of adults

Those who believe that screen violence can have a negative effect on children and young people often cite Albert Bandura's work as supporting evidence. In reality, it is quite hard to prove one way or another, although there are some well-known examples where exposure to violent images may well have played a part in violent behaviour. One such example is the murder in 1993 of 2-year-old Jamie Bulger in Liverpool. The case was widely reported and reacted to with horror as it became apparent that the toddler had been deliberately taken and killed by two 10-year-old boys. During the trial, it emerged that the boys had been watching films of a violent nature and there was some speculation that one particular film called *Child's Play*, in which a doll kills a child, may have influenced them.

The trial of the boys prompted the commissioning of two reports looking at the research evidence available. Whilst both reports suggested that video violence might have some effects on behaviour, both came to the conclusion that it would be difficult to say it was the actual cause of aggressive acts. Both reports did, however, comment upon the importance of stability and non-aggression in children's home lives. Research also concludes that realistic violence, which children and young people can identify with, is more harmful than cartoon violence. This would make sense, as generations of children have watched cartoons such as *Tom and Jerry* without problems.

- From your observations of children, do you see the influences that television and films might have on them?

- Do you remember watching any screened violence as a child? How did you react?

Intelligence

Intelligence testing, or variations of it, has become part of the testing procedures in most primary and secondary schools. Results from tests are often used for target-setting for teachers and pupils. This leads to interesting questions about how useful such testing is and whether intelligence can be measured effectively.

The history of intelligence tests

The first intelligence tests were devised by Alfred Binet and Theodore Simon in France in the early 1900s to detect children who would not cope with traditional schooling. In the US, the original tests were adapted and a scoring system was used called Intelligence Quotient, abbreviated to the more familiar 'IQ', which compares children's performance on the test against children of the same age.

In England in the 1940s, intelligence tests were used to work out which children would benefit from different types of education. The tests were known as the '11+'. Around 20 per cent of children who took the 11+ were given places at grammar schools where the curriculum was more abstract and academic, e.g. Latin, pure maths and physics were taught. From the introduction of the 11+ to the present day, there has been controversy. Firstly, boys generally did not perform as well as girls, so the scores had to be manipulated in order to make sure that a sufficient number of boys had places at grammar schools. Secondly, there was some concern that children's education and potential to gain qualifications were dependent on a single day's performance. It was argued that the 11+ did not take into account factors such as development and maturity. Interestingly, some of those children who 'failed' the 11+ went on to have very successful careers and businesses.

The validity of intelligence test results

The original intelligence tests were designed to detect children who would not cope in school, but often today they are thought of as having the power to detect underlying potential. This is not the case as, for example, a child who has not been exposed to language will not score well in verbal reasoning, whilst a child who has significant experience of numbers, patterns and shapes will perform better than a child who has little experience.

Performance in intelligence tests can also be affected by illness, stress, emotional disturbance and by familiarity. Thus children who are frequently tested often show some improvement in their scores as they become better at taking the test. However, intelligence scores for individuals seem to be fairly stable, especially in older children and young people, although at primary level there can be some fluctuation. Also, intelligence tests do seem to be fair predictors of children's and young people's overall achievement in school. Children with higher scores tend to do better than children with lower scores. This is, of course, related to the way in which they are testing skills that are required in order to achieve in a school situation. It is worth remembering here that intelligence tests are not able to predict emotional stability, happiness or future earnings!

Statistics

Cognitive ability tests

Today, in nearly two thirds of secondary schools, pupils sit cognitive ability tests (CATs). These tests are designed to assess reasoning skills and act as a way of predicting results in future achievement tests such as GCSEs.

'The Cognitive Abilities Test 3 (CAT3) is the most widely used test of reasoning abilities in the UK. Used to understand individual pupil potential and learning styles, CAT will help to inform your decision-making and target-setting.'

Source: NFER Nelson website (August 2006)

Nature or nurture

There are significant differences between the intelligence scores of groups of children based on their social class and their parents' level of income and education. This, again, prompts the nature or nurture debate in cognitive development. As one might expect, the answer is not clear cut and it is probable that both are likely to be at work. The following environmental variables have been found to influence intelligence test results.

- **Poverty** Children who come from low-income families tend to do less well in intelligence tests. This is a complex area, but poverty is associated with poorer nutrition and health, which can both affect brain development and growth. Poverty is also associated with higher rates of depression in parents and this can impact on the ability of parents to interact with their children.

- **Birth order** A slight, but not large, difference in IQ scores is seen between the oldest and subsequent children in a family. There is speculation that the oldest child in the family may benefit from having more one-to-one attention.

- **Parenting and family interactions** The way that parents interact and the environment they provide also seems to have an effect.

- **Pre-school and schooling** Early childhood experiences and schooling make a difference in IQ scores. This may be a result of children gaining the experiences, concepts and language that will help them achieve in intelligence tests.

> **Did you know?**
>
> IQ scores have been rising since testing began, thought to be a result of improved access to schooling, better nutrition and a society which is faster moving and creates more demands on the brain.

Are boys better at map-reading?

Overall, intelligence scores between boys and girls show no particular differences but, when different parts of the tests are analysed, there are some striking differences. Boys seem to perform better at spatial tasks, but particularly those that require some mental rotation. These are tasks where cubes or shapes need to be mentally manipulated. Differences are slight in young children but become more obvious later. It is important to stress that this is a general picture because, on an individual basis, some girls do well on spatial tasks whilst some boys do badly.

▲ Boys often, but not always, have better spatial skills than girls

The reasons why boys generally seem to be better on these tasks are hotly disputed, and once again the nature versus nurture debate rears its head. Some believe that these gender differences are biological ones, with hormones produced by the mother in pregnancy affecting brain development. Others believe that it is a result of boys' play preferences and that the way they play stimulates and strengthens the appropriate neural connections in the brain. Boys' toys often include a construction element and many boys are interested in mechanical structures and using computers.

Testing and the self-fulfilling prophecy

In the UK, children are being assessed or tested earlier and more frequently than at any time in the past. At the time of writing, children in England, for example, are assessed at the end of their reception year using the Foundation Stage profile and then again at ages 7, 11 and 14 years using Standard Attainment Tests, known as SAT tests. The original aim of SAT tests was to measure a school's performance, although the results of both the Foundation Stage profile and SAT tests are often used to set targets for schools. In addition, many primary schools and secondary school also use CAT tests (see page 132).

Whilst there may be benefits to assessing children, it is important to remember that teachers' expectations have been shown to have a significant impact on children's and young people's achievements in the classroom. A classic, and since replicated, experiment was carried out in the US in 1968 by Rosenthal and Jacobson. At the start of the academic year, teachers were given names of children who researchers told them had 'latent potential'. It was suggested that these children would show academic promise in the coming year. In reality, the names were taken at random but the results were startling. Overall, all pupils in the class did better than expected, but those children whose names had been identified made significant gains.

The effect that this experiment shows is known as the 'self-fulfilling prophecy', i.e. it shows that adults' expectations of children's behaviour and performance can influence how well children actually do. Therefore, testing benefits children whose results are strong, as teachers will assume that they are capable. The converse is true of children whose results are average, or below average, because teachers may not have such high expectations of them. These children and young people may, of course, simply have had an off day due to stress or, if we take brain development into account, had not yet completed neural growth.

> **Research it!**
>
> Explore the relationship between intelligence testing and brain development.
>
> ■ Compare the ages at which children and young people in the UK are tested to marked periods of growth within the brain.
>
> ■ Consider whether this may have an impact on children's and young people's test scores.

Other approaches to intelligence

Two notable theories have suggested that the current ways of measuring intelligence are limited and do not reflect the real world. Both theories suggest that intelligence is much broader and complex than what is tested in standard intelligence tests.

Sternberg's triarchic theory of intelligence

Sternberg suggests that intelligence falls broadly into three categories:

1. analytical intelligence
2. creative intelligence
3. practical intelligence.

He suggests that current intelligence tests and most achievement measured in schools only evaluate analytical intelligence.

Sternberg's theory (and that of Gardner's below) means that it could be argued that children and young people who are low on analytical intelligence but strong in, for example, practical intelligence are not being recognised in our current model of schooling and qualifications. Sternberg has produced his own intelligence test, which he claims measures all three types of intelligence.

Sternberg's three types of intelligence

Analytical intelligence
The ability to plan, organise and use information in new tasks, e.g. organising and planning what is required in order to submit coursework or working out the missing number in a pattern.

Practical intelligence
The ability to 'read' people and situations and to look for faster and easier ways of carrying out a task. Salespeople may adapt their selling style by 'reading' their customers, while an administration assistant may re-organise files to make their job quicker and easier.

Creative intelligence
The ability to find connections between existing ideas, products and materials. Creative intelligence results in inventions, as well as creative responses to problem-solving. For example, a designer may re-design the packaging of a product so that it is easier for the consumer to open.

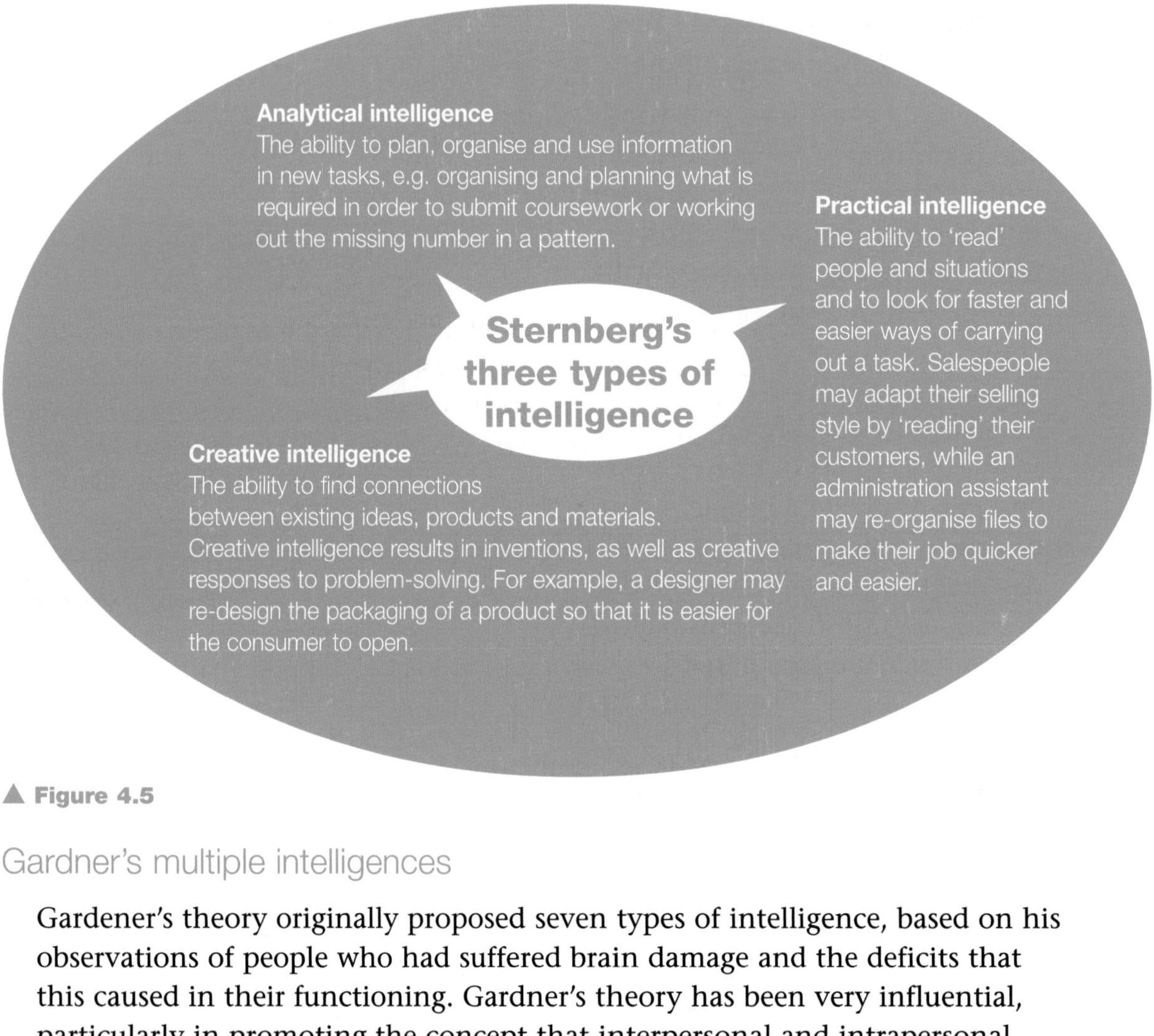

▲ Figure 4.5

Gardner's multiple intelligences

Gardener's theory originally proposed seven types of intelligence, based on his observations of people who had suffered brain damage and the deficits that this caused in their functioning. Gardner's theory has been very influential, particularly in promoting the concept that interpersonal and intrapersonal intelligence is essential. The term 'emotional intelligence' is now widely used in connection with these intelligences.

- **Linguistic** The ability to use language, write and also learn other languages; skills used by, for example, interpreters and journalists.

- **Logical/mathematical** The ability to manipulate numbers, find sequences and patterns and use logic to solve problems (required by scientists and engineers, etc.).

- **Musical** The ability to produce and compose music as well as to appreciate it (required by musicians and dancers, etc.).

- **Spatial** The ability to notice shapes, spaces and the relationship between objects (required by racing drivers and architects, etc.).

- **Bodily kinaesthetic** The ability to coordinate one's body movements skilfully (required by dancers and athletes, etc.).

- **Interpersonal** The ability to be aware of other's responses and needs (required by nurses and social workers, etc.).

- **Intrapersonal** The ability to be self-aware and reflective (required for self-discipline and controlling anger, etc.).

Differences in achievement rates between boys and girls

For the past few years, girls' achievement in schools has outstripped that of boys, which has led to some concern that boys might be underachieving. If the press is to be believed, this is a new phenomenon, but the reality is that girls have been outperforming boys at GCSE level since 1994 when there was a 9 per cent gap. Since 1994 this gap has been quite a stable one, although it has widened slightly to 10 per cent as Figure 4.6 shows. At 18, the gap is still there but is much narrower at around 2 per cent. Interestingly, in national curriculum tests, boys and girls seem to do equally well in maths and science, but there is a gap when it comes to English.

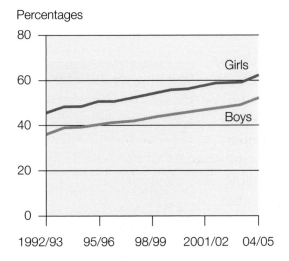
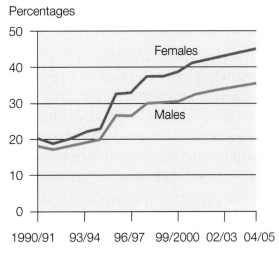

▲ **Figure 4.6** GCSE and A level results

Explanations for differences

There has been much speculation about why boys and girls are performing differently and it is probable that the reasons are complex. Some reasons that have been put forward are outlined below.

- **Changes to syllabus and course structure** It has been suggested that coursework alongside examinations benefits girls more than boys and also that the curriculum may be less appealing to boys.

- **Media and computer games** Since the 1990s, there are more opportunities to watch television, videos and DVDs. The advent of the computer, video games and the internet has also meant that children and young people are spending more time on activities, whilst there has been a decline in the amount of time spent reading. Boys are often identified as being more interested than girls in using new technology.

- **Role models and peer pressure** There is some speculation as to whether or not boys identify reading, studying and doing well at school with a positive self-image. It is thought that many boys' heroes are sporting ones rather than academic ones.

- **Reading methods** There is powerful speculation that the way that boys are being taught to read, using a mixed method, might not be effective. Advocates of this position believe that a system known as synthetic phonics should be used. Others believe that the system of beginning the process of reading at 5 years of age is too early and disadvantages boys. For information about reading methods and this debate visit the National Literacy Trust website, a link to which has been made available at www. heinemann.co.uk/hotlinks. Enter the express code 983XP.

Going to school

The majority of children in the UK attend school, although some children and young people are educated at home. The statutory starting age for school in the UK is the term after a child reaches 5 years old. In practice, however, many children will be attending full-time school when they are 4 years old. This is an earlier start than in many other countries, where the statutory start is often around 6 or 7 years old. Starting school is a major step in not only children's cognitive development but also, crucially, their emotional development, as they learn to cope within a larger group.

Research it!

Visit the Department for Education and Skills (DFES) website and look at statistics for National Curriculum tests, GCSEs and A levels. A link to this website has been made available at www.heinemann.co.uk/hotlinks. Enter the express code 983XP.

You can also interview parents and young people. Ask them about their perceptions of pass rates.

In the UK, there are four school curricula that reflect the character and aspirations of each of the home countries: Scotland, England, Northern Ireland and Wales. Whilst there are more similarities than differences in terms of structure and qualifications between England, Northern Ireland and Wales, there are major differences in Scotland. Below is a brief description of the National Curriculum as it stands in England. Note that England has been chosen only on the basis that it has the largest number of school-aged children in the UK.

▲ Going to school may aid not only a child's cognitive development but also their emotional development

National Curriculum: England

The National Curriculum was introduced as a way of ensuring that all children had access to similar knowledge and skills, regardless of the school they attended. For each Key Stage, there are compulsory subjects that have to be taught. The National Curriculum in England is divided into three Key Stages, which broadly reflect the infant, junior and early secondary schooling of children. In addition, there is also an earlier stage covering 0–5 years, which from 2008 will be known as the Early Years Foundation Stage.

National testing takes place at the end of each Key Stage in three subjects: English, science and mathematics. These are termed 'core' subjects. For each, there is a series of attainment levels that help define the skills and knowledge that children should have. Examples are shown in Tables 4.1 to 4.3.

Table 4.1 Age 5–7, Key Stage 1, expected level of attainment 2

Attainment	Expectation
Level 2 attainment target for writing	Pupils' writing communicates meaning in both narrative and non-narrative forms, using appropriate and interesting vocabulary, and showing some awareness of the reader. Ideas are developed in a sequence of sentences, sometimes demarcated by capital letters and full stops. Simple, monosyllabic words are usually spelt correctly and, where there are inaccuracies, the alternative is phonetically plausible. In handwriting, letters are accurately formed and consistent in size.
Level 2 attainment target for reading (source: National Curriculum QCA/DFES)	Pupils' reading of simple texts shows understanding and is generally accurate. They express opinions about major events or ideas in stories, poems and non-fiction. They use more than one strategy, such as phonic, graphic, syntactic and contextual, in reading unfamiliar words and establishing meaning.
Level 2 attainment target for mathematics	Pupils count sets of objects reliably, and use mental recall of addition and subtraction facts up to 10. They begin to understand the place value of each digit in a number and use this to order numbers up to 100. They choose the appropriate operation when solving addition and subtraction problems. They use the knowledge that subtraction is the inverse of addition. They use mental calculation strategies to solve number problems involving money and measures. They recognise sequences of numbers, including odd and even numbers.

Table 4.2 Age 7–11, Key Stage 2, expected level of attainment 4

Attainment	Expectation
Level 4 attainment target for writing	Pupils' writing in a range of forms is lively and thoughtful. Ideas are often sustained and developed in interesting ways and organised appropriately for the purpose of the reader. Vocabulary choices are often adventurous and words are used for effect. Pupils are beginning to use grammatically complex sentences, extending meaning. Spelling, including that of polysyllabic words that conform to regular patterns, is generally accurate. Full stops, capital letters and question marks are used correctly, and pupils are beginning to use punctuation within the sentence. Handwriting style is fluent, joined and legible.
Level 4 attainment target for reading (source: National Curriculum QCA/DFES)	In responding to a range of texts, pupils show understanding of significant ideas, themes, events and characters, beginning to use inference and deduction. They refer to the text when explaining their views. They locate and use ideas and information.
Level 4 attainment target for mathematics	Pupils use their understanding of place value to multiply and divide whole numbers by 10 or 100. In solving number problems, pupils use a range of mental methods of computation with the four operations, including mental recall of multiplication facts up to 10 x 10 and quick derivation of corresponding division facts. They use efficient written methods of addition and subtraction and of short multiplication and division. They add and subtract decimals to two places and order decimals to three places. In solving problems with or without a calculator, pupils check the reasonableness of their results by reference to their knowledge of the context or to the size of the numbers. They recognise approximate proportions of a whole and use simple fractions and percentages to describe these. Pupils recognise and describe number patterns, and relationships including multiple, factor and square. They begin to use simple formulae expressed in words. Pupils use and interpret coordinates in the first quadrant.

Table 4.3 Age 11–14, Key Stage 3, expected level of attainment 5–6

Attainment	Expectation
Level 5 attainment target for writing	Pupils' writing is varied and interesting, conveying meaning clearly in a range of forms for different readers, using a more formal style where appropriate. Vocabulary choices are imaginative and words are used precisely. Simple and complex sentences are organised into paragraphs. Words with complex regular patterns are usually spelt correctly. A range of punctuation, including commas, apostrophes and inverted commas, is usually used accurately. Handwriting is joined, clear and fluent and, where appropriate, is adapted to a range of tasks.
Level 5 attainment target for reading (source: National Curriculum QCA/DFES)	Pupils show understanding of a range of texts, selecting essential points and using inference and deduction where appropriate. In their responses, they identify key features, themes and characters and select sentences, phrases and relevant information to support their views. They retrieve and collate information from a range of sources.
Level 5 attainment target for mathematics	Pupils use their understanding of place value to multiply and divide whole numbers and decimals by 10, 100 and 1000. They order, add and subtract negative numbers in context. They use all four operations with decimals to two places. They reduce a fraction to its simplest form by cancelling common factors and solve simple problems involving ratio and direct proportion. They calculate fractional or percentage parts of quantities and measurements, using a calculator where appropriate. Pupils understand and use an appropriate non-calculator method for solving problems that involve multiplying and dividing any three-digit number by any two-digit number. They check their solutions by applying inverse operations or estimating using approximations. They construct, express in symbolic form and use simple formulae involving one or two operations. They use brackets appropriately. Pupils use and interpret coordinates in all four quadrants.

Learning to read and write

One of the major tasks that children face is to learn to read and write. This is considered to be essential in a literate society where most employers see this as a basic skill.

The story so far...
Early development of reading and writing skills

The starting point for learning to read and write is language. Children need to be using language in speech well in order to be ready to make sense of language in print. Research also shows that children who have strong phonological awareness (i.e. differentiating between sounds) also master reading more quickly. This means that learning nursery rhymes or playing games such as 'I spy' are crucial before formal teaching of reading. Children also need to have developed a love of books, and so children who have enjoyed sharing books and hearing stories are likely to do well.

Handwriting is a fine motor skill that children need to develop early on so that they can put down their words on paper. Later on in schools, children are encouraged to type and by the end of the secondary phase, most work that is handed in is typewritten. The development of fine motor skills and hand-eye coordination can be promoted by activities such as threading, painting and construction.

Reading

Reading is a complex skill and young readers are often employing more than one strategy in order to read. Three approaches to reading are summarised in Figure 4.7.

Reading is more than just decoding

An important part of reading is comprehension. This is why the level of children's overall language when they learn to read is so important. Children who do not understand the meaning of the words that they are reading are likely to find the task of reading slow and boring. When first learning to read, children are given books with pictures. The pictures help them to understand what is happening in the text and so make the reading more pleasurable. The move towards text with no pictures can be hard for children whose language skills are poor. The words that they have decoded may not conjure images in their imagination and so may prevent them from enjoying or understanding what is happening.

Research it!

- Which method helped you learn to read?

- Find out more about the current debate on reading methods. A useful place to start is the National Literacy Trust website. Visit www.heinemann.co.uk/hotlinks for a link to the site. Simply enter the express code 983XP.

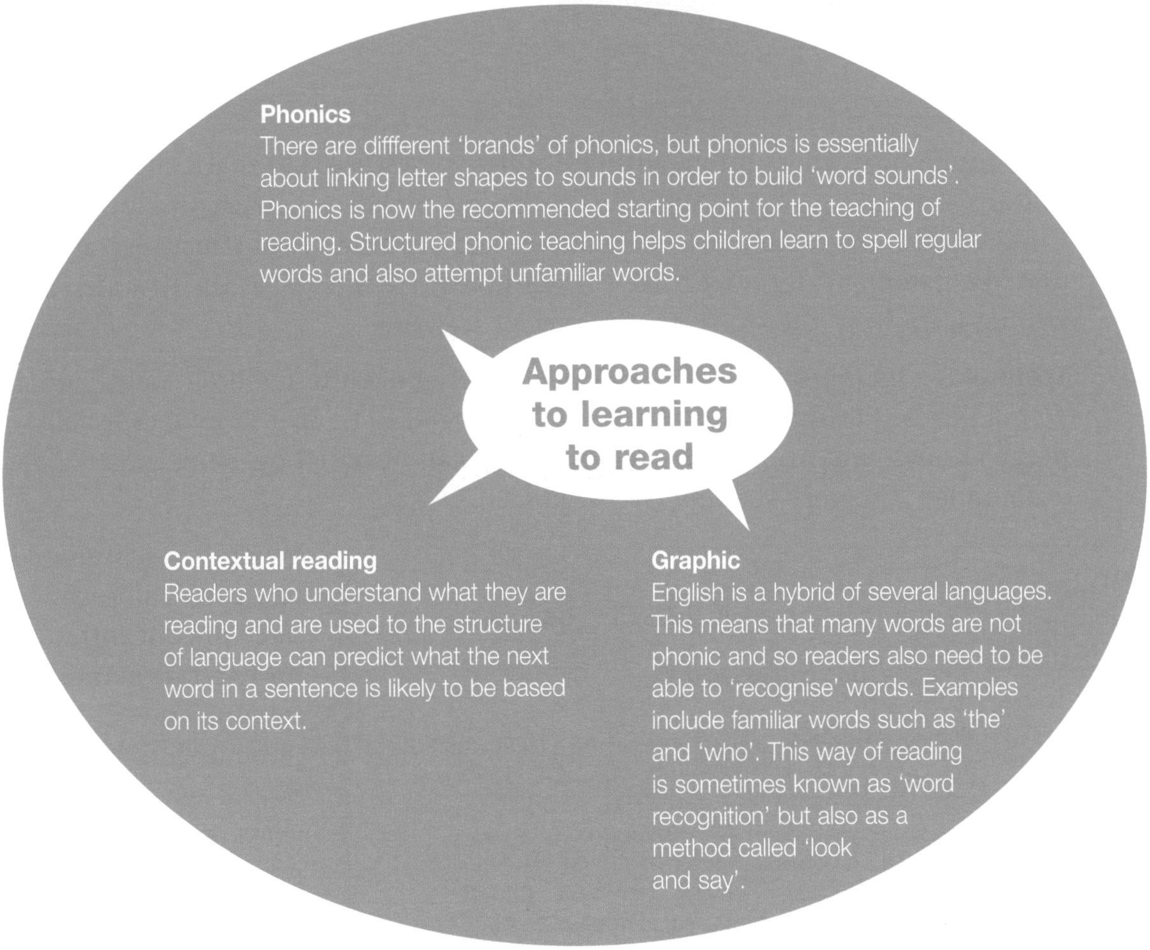

Phonics
There are diffferent 'brands' of phonics, but phonics is essentially about linking letter shapes to sounds in order to build 'word sounds'. Phonics is now the recommended starting point for the teaching of reading. Structured phonic teaching helps children learn to spell regular words and also attempt unfamiliar words.

Approaches to learning to read

Contextual reading
Readers who understand what they are reading and are used to the structure of language can predict what the next word in a sentence is likely to be based on its context.

Graphic
English is a hybrid of several languages. This means that many words are not phonic and so readers also need to be able to 'recognise' words. Examples include familiar words such as 'the' and 'who'. This way of reading is sometimes known as 'word recognition' but also as a method called 'look and say'.

▲ Figure 4.7

Functional readers

Whilst reading is given great prominence in schools, children over the past few years have been reading less and less. Fewer children now read for pleasure than ever before and there has been an increase in 'functional readers'. These are readers who are capable of reading, but only do so for a definite purpose, such as finding out information or completing a task for school. Functional readers prefer non-fiction and can find it hard to concentrate on extended text.

The move away from reading for pleasure has been linked to more opportunities to gain information, entertainment and enjoyment from more visual media forms, such as computers, films and television. Some commentators have blamed the way in which English is taught, suggesting that it is too analytical and puts children and young people off. Overall, in terms of reading trends, the amount of time spent reading declines as children move from primary into secondary school.

Did you know?

One in ten children and young people say that they do not like reading very much.

Writing

Learning to turn words into a written format is another skill that children need to learn. Again, it is closely linked to children's spoken language development. Children who have extensive vocabularies and are able to construct sentences that are grammatically correct have a significant advantage, as the first step in writing is to 'hear' the words that you want to write.

Spelling is a major ingredient in writing, closely linked to children's and young people's reading skills. Some spellings need to be memorised, especially irregular ones, and mastery of these spellings can be aided by using the 'elaboration' memory strategy (see page 120).

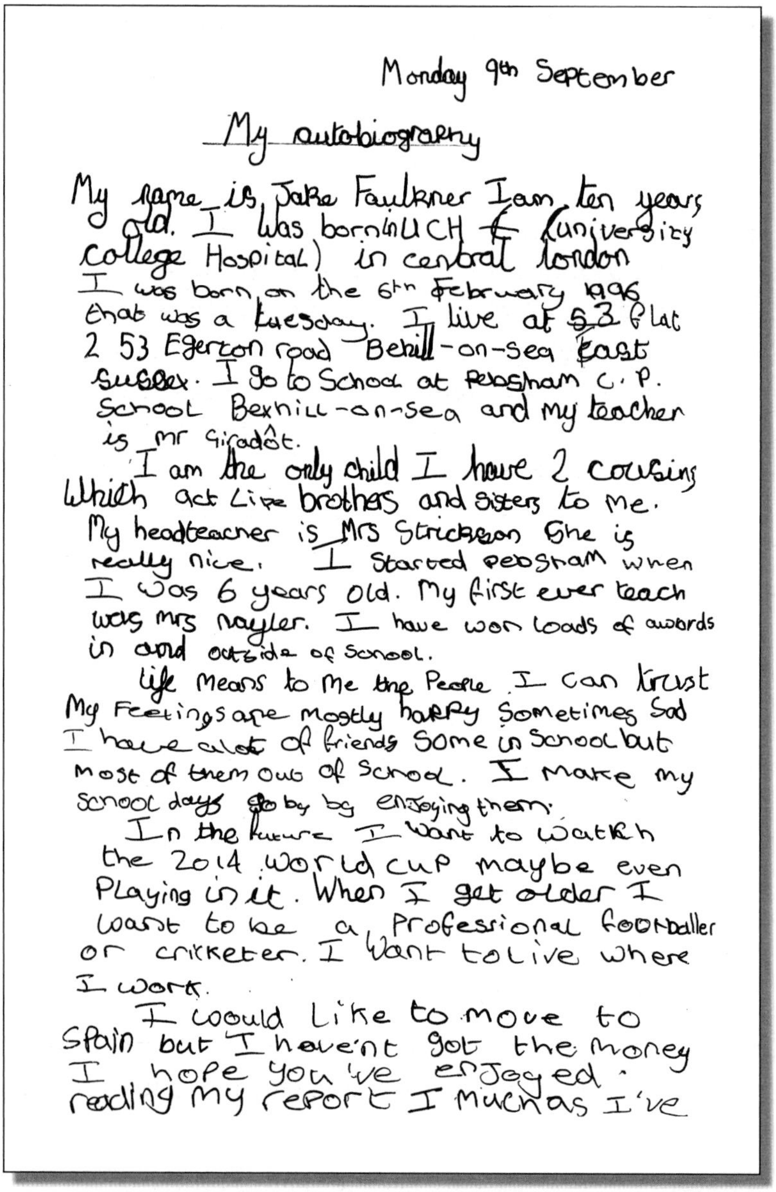

When first learning to write, children have to concentrate on letter formation, spelling and punctuation, but by the age of 8 years or so the process of writing is usually easier and faster. However, expectations of the quantity of writing that children should be able to produce increase as they get older, and it is from this point onwards that children and young people who 'do not have a lot to say' may find writing difficult.

▲ **Figure 4.8** An example of an 11-year-old's handwriting

▲ Dyslexia can make learning to read and write difficult

Dyslexia

Whilst most children are able to learn to read and write without much problem, some children have enormous problems, particularly with reading and spelling. The term often used to describe this problem is dyslexia, although this is very much an 'umbrella' term. Children who are recognised as having dyslexia often have difficulties in remembering the link between sounds and letter shapes, and may not recognise words that they have read earlier. Learning to read is therefore a slow and arduous process. Spelling is difficult too and sometimes letters in their handwriting are jumbled up. They may also have difficulty with their handwriting, in organising themselves and in concentrating for long periods, despite trying very hard.

Causes of dyslexia

The causes of dyslexia are still unclear, although there are several strands of research which all suggest that something neurological is occurring.

- Firstly, there may be a genetic component as dyslexia does tend to run in families.

- A second area of interest is diet, with some children appearing to benefit from a change of diet. This usually involves children avoiding processed foods and increasing the vitamin, mineral and omega-3 content of their food.

- A third area of research looks at the links between dyslexia and difficulties with coordination and balance, as these are also apparent in some dyslexic children.

- Finally, there is research that looks at the difficulties that children may have in processing sounds and breaking them down.

Interview – *Ruth, 23 years old*

Q. How did your school treat your dyslexia?

A. When I was about 9, I remember being taken out of classes and put in small groups with others and being talked to as if we were stupid. I remember being frustrated because I couldn't pick things up as quickly as others and being aware of others doing it easily. They talked to me as if I was stupid, but I wasn't though.

Q. How did your experience make you feel?

A. I was really embarrassed about it. Learning support class came in and got me and I was really embarrassed that everyone knew. I had a tutor on Saturday mornings because the way she talked to me was better. She was understanding. I learnt so much from her.

Helping a child with dyslexia

Children with dyslexia can become very disheartened to find that they cannot pick up reading as quickly as others. This can mean that, very slowly, children with dyslexia give up and look for ways of avoiding reading or spelling. As the gap widens between themselves and other children, so too does their level of self-esteem. Recognising that a child has a difficulty early on is therefore essential, as there are specialist programmes and support available.

What does it mean in practice?

Supporting children and young people with dyslexia

- Praise them for the effort they are putting in.
- Plan small steps of learning. Repeat and reinforce in many ways.
- Check on previous learning before continuing.
- Use as many sensory techniques as possible when supporting reading, writing or spelling.
- Write words and sentences in different colours so that they are more noticeable, especially if anything has to be copied.
- Allow more time for tasks, but notice when concentration is flagging.
- Avoid continually correcting written work or reading. Focus on some key points that are within reach.
- Focus on the positive when marking.
- Help them remember spellings or the written shapes of sounds by linking them to stories. Ask them to think about how they might find a way of remembering them.
- Tell children and young people about successful adults who have managed to cope with their dyslexia.
- Use computer-assisted technology to enable children and young people to enjoy writing.

Research it!

Find out more about supporting children with dyslexia. The internet is a useful starting point. Links to some useful sites have been made available at www.heinemann.co.uk/hotlinks. Simply enter the express code 983XP.

Learning mathematics

As well as the emphasis on reading and writing, children and young people are also expected to be numerate. Ironically, it is often one area where adults have great difficulty and where, as we will see, attitudes towards this as a subject area are quite negative.

The story so far...

Early development of numeracy

The major task in children's earliest years is to learn the meaning of number, as well as the actual labels such as 'one' and 'two'. This is important, as some children are able to count aloud but can neither count objects accurately nor understand that 10 is a number larger than 5. For most children, this basic understanding of number comes when they are around 4 or 5 years old. Grouping objects, sorting and matching are therefore activities that children need to master before they can begin to formally record numbers.

Abstract reasoning and mathematics

Piaget's theory of cognitive development (see page 109) has much relevance when it comes to mathematics. He suggested that children under 7 years of age benefit from actually handling objects when adding or subtracting and carrying out other simple mathematical tasks. Whilst older children can do some simple abstract tasks, they too often benefit from seeing or experiencing the task first in a more 'concrete' way. Thus a game where children collect tokens and, when they have collected ten, can convert them into a voucher may help children understand the decimal system. Playing the game provides them with an experience that they can use as a basis for abstract tasks.

Whilst many children perform relatively well in the primary phase, significant differences between children emerge during the secondary phase of schooling. This might be expected in light of Piaget's work. He was clear that not all young people would be able to use 'formal operations' (see page 112 for more about formal operations). Secondary school mathematics becomes increasingly abstract and distant from young people's immediate experiences. For some young people this is a huge problem and may account for the increasing gap between mathematical abilities of young people.

Mathematics and information processing

Numeracy strategy advocates the learning by memory of 'number facts' and also the use of mental mathematics. Number facts are things like multiplication tables and number bonds such as 8 + 7 = 15. This approach is thought to be beneficial, as it can free up information-processing space in the brain. It is also important for more complex mathematical tasks, which require you to 'hold' a piece of information whilst working on another, e.g. $(24 - 9) + (32 \times 6)$.

Confidence and expectations

As well as cognitive explanations of why some children may not do well at mathematics, there are also emotional and social ones. Confidence is one of the major keys to learning. With mathematics, some children develop a fear that they will be unable to do it. Thus, when faced with a new mathematical concept, they are likely to become stressed. The effect of stress, in turn, limits the brain's capacity to focus and remember, increasing the probability that a child may not understand the new concept. A vicious cycle is quickly entered into, where the fear of mathematics becomes a real barrier to any new learning.

The need for children to be confident, as well as the importance of memory, is one reason why countries that have high success rates in teaching mathematics tend to have very structured systems, where repetition plays a key part along with frequent re-visiting of previous concepts. Social expectations and attitudes towards mathematics also play a part. In this country, many view mathematics as an innate ability, rather than a skill that can be practised. Parents, children and even some teachers believe that being born 'good at it' or with a 'mathematical mind' is more important than working hard. These attitudes are in direct contrast to Japan, where parents and teachers see practice and working hard as the most important factors in gaining mathematical competency. A self-fulfilling prophecy is therefore likely to be a major factor in the differences between mathematical ability in Japan and the UK.

Drawing diagrams

- Construct graphs and diagrams to represent data
- Interpret graphs and diagrams and draw inferences

Key words
time series
pie charts
frequency diagram
frequency polygon

It is important to choose the most suitable diagram for a data set.

Evaluate results → Specify the problem and plan → Collect data from a variety of sources → Process and represent data → Interpret and discuss data

Time series are useful for plotting data that varies over time, for example temperatures and populations.

Pie charts are useful for categorical data, where the categories are percentages or parts of a whole.

You can show the overall shape of a distribution by joining the midpoints of a **frequency diagram** with straight lines. This is called a **frequency polygon**. You can easily compare two distributions by looking at the frequency polygons.

Example

Two frequency polygons are drawn to show the heights of 100 13-year old boys and girls.

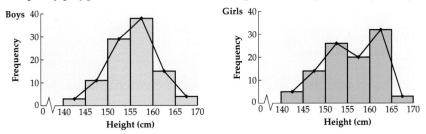

a) Draw the two frequency polygons as a superimposed frequency polygon.

b) Jane has read that the average 13-year old girl is taller than the average 13-year old boy. Does this diagram support this? What other information does Jane need to decide if this is true?

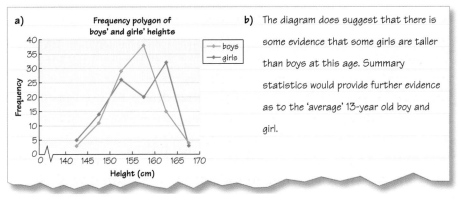

a) Frequency polygon of boys' and girls' heights

b) The diagram does suggest that there is some evidence that some girls are taller than boys at this age. Summary statistics would provide further evidence as to the 'average' 13-year old boy and girl.

▲ **Figure 4.9** A page from a mathematics textbook for Year 9 students

Chapter 4 Cognitive development

What does it mean in practice?

Supporting children and young people who are learning mathematics

■ Have positive expectations for children and young people in terms of mathematics.

■ Avoid negative messages such as 'Some people are just born good at it!'

■ Look for ways of making a mathematical concept 'real' or relevant.

■ Provide plenty of practice material so that children and young people can feel that they have mastered an aspect of mathematics.

■ Use games as a way of encouraging the learning of concepts and also to practise number facts.

■ Show how mathematics is used in many aspects of daily living.

■ Give children and young people sufficient time when working out problems.

■ Avoid focusing on wrong answers, instead encouraging children to work out whether their answer to a problem is logical.

Show your knowledge

1. Why is neural pruning a significant element of brain development?

2. Why might it be beneficial for children to work together on tasks requiring thought?

3. Explain the importance of language in cognitive development.

4. What is meant by the term 'positive reinforcer'?

5. How does the social cognitive learning theory explain children's learning?

6. Identify three different strategies that might be used to memorise information.

7. Discuss the limitations of intelligence testing.

8. How does language link to the process of learning to read and write?

9. List three ways in which you might support a child with dyslexia.

10. Explain how attitudes towards mathematics might affect attainment.

Chapter 5

Physical development

Physical development plays an extraordinarily important part in children's and young people's lives, alongside some of the issues associated with physical development, such as nutrition and physical activity. This chapter begins by looking at physical development and puberty and goes on to consider the influences on growth and health.

This chapter is divided into the following sections:

- The importance of growth and physical development
- Puberty
- Nutrition
- Physical activity
- Smoking
- Drug and alcohol use

The importance of growth and physical development

The way in which children grow and develop physical skills has a significant impact not only on their learning, but also on the way in which they and others see themselves. Tall children, for example, are likely to find that adults have greater expectations of them, which mostly leads to positive outcomes as they develop strong feelings of self-efficacy. In the same way, children who can control their physical movements very well are more likely to be able to take part in more complex games or be able to do more things for themselves, and so again develop positive feelings about their capabilities.

Many skills that are valued in education are often linked to physical development, although this is not always recognised. Handwriting is linked to fine motor skills, whilst sitting still is also a physically complex task involving balance and high levels of co-ordination! Later in childhood, when hormones begin the physical changes of puberty, children's and young people's self-images undergo a change too. The physical transformation from child to adult is not necessarily a smooth one, as we will see, so can easily affect self-esteem.

Growth

One of the phrases that generally pleases young children, but increasingly annoys young people is 'Haven't you grown?' Growth is a major feature of childhood and one that children recognise early on. New shoes and clothes are visible ways of recognising that growth has taken place.

The story so far...

Growth and development in early childhood

Significant amounts of growth take place in a child's first two years of life. By 2 years old they will have reached half of their expected adult height. They have also tripled their birth weight. From 2 years onwards, the rate of both height and weight gain slows down until adolescence.

Incredible progress is also made in the first few years in the development of physical skills. More deliberate and controlled movements have replaced some of the early reflexes, e.g. the 'startle' reflex. Children are usually walking by 18 months and can use their hands to pick up and pass objects and toys. At 5 years old, the list of physical skills that children have mastered is considerable and usually includes dressing and toileting, as well as using a tricycle.

Factors affecting growth

Children's rates of growth are linked to the production of hormones, including thyroxine secreted from the thyroid and growth hormone secreted from the pituitary gland. The pituitary gland is a key gland in terms of hormone production, and for this reason is sometimes dubbed the 'master gland'. It not only produces hormones that affect the body directly, but also produces hormones that are sent to other glands as messengers. Once received, these glands go on to produce further hormones. Thyroxine is a good example of this, as it is produced only when the thyroid receives a 'messenger' from the pituitary.

The overall height and build of a child are also linked to other factors, especially genetic ones. Children usually follow a similar pattern of growth and development to their parents, although there are obviously some exceptions. In addition, there are important environmental factors that can affect a child's growth and development.

▶
A child's growth and final adult height are influenced by many factors

As well as nutrition and exercise (see pages 166 and 173), sleep is another very important factor affecting growth. Sleep seems to be important for cognitive function and general health but also for growth, as it is during sleep that the pituitary gland secretes growth hormones. This is one reason why, at times of growth, children and young people will often seem to sleep well. A good example of this is during the teenage years, where young people will often need at least nine hours of sleep in comparison to many adults who are fine with seven or less. This is perhaps one reason why young people are known to infuriate their parents by lying in bed until late!

Interview – *Baran, 14 years old*

I am in school where there are a lot of boys taller than me. Sometimes they tease me and push me around in the corridor. I am not the only one in my class. There are about five of us, but I still don't like it. I keep measuring myself to see if I have grown. There is one boy in my class and he looks really old. Sometimes visitors to the school think he is one of the teachers. He doesn't like that either.

What does it mean in practice?

How adult behaviour is affected by the outward appearance of children and young people

Adults often focus on the appearance of children and young people when thinking about expectations of behaviour and levels of maturity. Those children and young people who are either tall or short for their age may, therefore, be treated differently. This means that it is important to be careful not to make assumptions based on appearance and be thoughtful about comments that are made. It is also important to consider whether a child's or young person's height is affecting their confidence.

Stamina

Stamina is the ability of the body to sustain physical activity. It is linked to lung capacity and the cardiovascular system.

The story so far...

Stamina in young children

Toddlers and pre-school children often move and run in short bursts. They find it difficult to go for long walks, but will happily run a little and then clamber to sit in a pushchair. The heart rate of toddlers and pre-school children is higher than adults as their lungs and hearts are smaller.

Stamina development 6–11 years

As children's hearts and lungs grow, they are able to sustain activity levels for slightly longer periods, although the need to rest frequently remains. This means that most 10-year-olds will be able to maintain physical activity for longer periods than 6-year-olds, but both age ranges will still need resting periods. Endurance types of activity, such as long-distance running, are not usually appropriate for this age range because of developing stamina levels.

During this age range, boys' and girls' stamina levels are similar, with boys having the slight edge. There are, of course, individual differences partly dependent on physical build, weight and exercise levels.

Stamina development 12–16 years

During adolescence, stamina levels increase dramatically. This is because of the growth spurt that takes place as part of puberty. There are marked differences between the stamina, speed and strength of boys and girls. Boys are stronger and also able to sustain physical activity for longer periods.

What does it mean in practice?

Matching activity to age and development

It is important that activities are suitable for the age and development stage of children for them to be enjoyable. This is particularly important as the amount of exercise that children and young people are taking has been in decline (see section on exercise page 173).

- Plan 'stop and start' types of activity for children under the age of 11 years.

- Look out for signs that a child is tired, e.g. face colour, breathlessness.

- Think about the fitness levels of individual children and young people when planning games and activities.

- Allow children to rest as they need, without any stigma being attached.

Observing theory

■ Watch children aged 6–11 years running around. Keep a note of their rest and activity patterns. Are there any significant differences between boys and girls?

■ Repeat the observation but, this time, watch young people aged 12 and over. What are the differences in activity levels? Are there differences between boys and girls?

Fat and muscles

Fat tissue and muscle fibres are part of every body's make up, although there are differences between boys and girls from birth that particularly show themselves during adolescence. Girls are born with more fat tissue and, throughout childhood, have a higher fat ratio than boys. The difference is more accentuated during adolescence when the fat makes up around 24 per cent of a girl's weight as opposed to around 14 per cent of a boy's.

The converse is true for muscle mass. Boys have more muscle mass than girls and this is, again, particularly noticeable during adolescence. Sex hormones are thought to be the reason behind the difference, as even girls who take plenty of exercise will not be as strong as boys of the same age.

▶ The increased muscle mass of males is usually evident even in quite young boys

The need for accurate information about puberty

Puberty is a time when the self-concept of both boys and girls has to accommodate a new body shape. Many girls become worried about their body shape. It is, therefore, helpful to provide accurate information about the changes that will take place as they go through puberty, but also ways in which they can eat well and take exercise.

Gross and fine motor development

Gross and fine motor movements help us to use our bodies and carry out tasks. Gross motor movements involve the whole limb, whilst fine motor movements are the small movements usually associated with the hands.

The story so far...
Early development of motor movement

The first five years of life are incredible in terms of fine and gross motor movement development. By the age of 5, most children are able to climb, run and cycle, and control all of their gross motor movements well. Fine motor movements are slighter slower to develop, but, still, by 5 years of age most children can thread beads easily, draw pictures and use a knife and fork. This development is, however, dependent on children being given encouragement and opportunities to play and use equipment. Thus a child who is not given a tricycle will not learn how to pedal and steer.

Did you know?

One in fourteen children is left handed

Motor movement development 6–11 years

Whilst children under 6 years have some control over their gross and fine motor skills, there continues to be further development that is particularly noticeable in respect of their fine motor skills. Handwriting is easier to join up and becomes smaller, drawings become more detailed and the amount of effort required to master such tasks is considerably less. Fine motor development and coordination are related to brain development and growth (see section on brain development in Chapter 4 Cognitive development, page 104).

Motor movement development 12–16 years

Ossification of the bones in the hands and wrists is completed during the teenage years. This results in increased strength, so most teenagers will find it easy to open a screw lid jar, whilst younger children will often find it difficult. The perceptual skills of young people are now more developed and combine with gross and fine motor skills, resulting in greater physical sophistication. Games, such as rounders or tennis, become easier and playing computer games becomes simpler.

> **Did you know?**
>
> Ossification refers to the depositing of layers of hard bone tissue by special cells called osteoblasts, which give bones their strength.

Puberty

The process of moving into adulthood is marked by physical changes to the body. It is a complex process involving a series of different hormones, which produce a range of chemical interactions. These are listed in Table 5.1.

> **Did you know?**
>
> Puberty usually takes 4–5 years.

Table 5.1 **Key hormones involved in growth and puberty**

Hormone	Gland	Effects
Thyroxine	Thyroid	Rate of growth and brain development. Secreted in significant amounts in first two years of life.
Adrenal androgen	Adrenal	Affects growth, especially in girls during puberty. Interacts with other hormones. Responsible for strength in muscles and bones.
Testosterone	Testes	Produced in significant quantities in boys from the age of around 11 years onwards. Responsible for sexual development, but also triggers further release of growth hormone.
Oestradiol	Ovaries	One of the sex hormones in girls. Responsible for breast development, pubic hair growth and menstrual cycle.
Growth hormone	Pituitary	Responsible for growth and physical maturation.
Gonadotrophic hormones	Pituitary	Hormones produced by the pituitary as messengers to the ovaries in girls and the testes in boys. As a result they respectively produce oestrogens and testosterone.
Luteinising hormone (LH)	Pituitary	Regulates the menstrual cycle.
Follicle stimulating hormone (FSH)	Pituitary	Stimulates the ovaries to produce an ovum.

The pituitary gland begins the process of puberty by producing hormones that stimulate further hormone production in the testes and ovaries. In boys, the key hormone is testosterone whilst in girls it is the oestrogens, notably oestradiol. These hormones result in changes to the key sexual organs, usually referred to as primary sex characteristics. In girls, there are changes to the ovaries, uterus and vagina, whilst in boys there are changes to the penis and testes.

As well as primary sex characteristics, hormones also change the physical appearance of boys and girls. These changes are known as secondary sex characteristics and include pubic hair development in both sexes, as well as breast development in girls and change in voice pitch in boys. The physical transformation from child to adult usually takes place over four or five years, although, as with other areas of development, there can be variations between individuals.

Girls

Puberty begins earlier in girls than in boys and follows a definite sequence, although the timing can vary considerably between individuals. The starting point is changes in the breasts when the nipples begin to protrude or 'bud' and is often seen in 10- and 11-year-olds. This is followed by initial growth of the pubic hair and then a significant growth spurt.

The growth spurt is usually followed by the first period, known as the 'menarche'. At this point few girls are fertile and it takes some time before periods become regular and fertility is fully established. In terms of timing, the majority of girls will start their periods between the ages of 11 and 15, with 12–14 seen as the 'optimum' time by girls themselves (see below). The physical transformation is often completed by 17 years of age, although, as with all areas of physical development, this is only a guide.

Did you know?

Ninety-five per cent of girls start their periods between the ages of 11 and 15.

Self-esteem and puberty amongst girls

Whilst puberty would appear, on the surface, to be about physical transformations, in reality it can significantly affect emotional development too. Girls who develop earlier than their peers are more likely to have low self-esteem, poor body image and tend to do less well in school. It would seem that timing is all important when it comes to puberty and even a slight variation can make girls feel less positive about themselves.

Most girls, it would appear, have their own 'schedule' as to when they wish to start their periods, and the optimum time seems to be 12–14 years of age. The medical definition of 'precocious puberty' is the onset of periods before the age of 10. Thus 11-year-olds, who may feel that they have started 'too early', are not considered to be exceptional, although this indeed is what they may feel.

So what about those whose puberty is at the late end of normative development? Whilst this too is problematic in terms of self-esteem, it seems to have less overall impact than starting early. Interestingly, the converse is true for boys (see below).

As part of the process of puberty, girls also have to come to terms with changing body shape. Increased body fat and breast development, which may not fit in with a girl's 'ideal' body shape, seem to create pressures. This may be one of the reasons why girls' scores of self-esteem seem to dip during adolescence.

> **Did you know?**
>
> Girls today menstruate earlier than ever before. In 1840, the average age of menarche was 17.

Boys

The start of puberty in boys begins with initial pubic hair growth and genital development. The timing varies between boys, but is likely to occur at around 11 years of age. This is followed by a sharp growth spurt, alongside continued development of the testes and penis.

Growth, in terms of height, often continues until boys are 18. The voice deepens or 'breaks' after this initial burst of growth, so that many boys by 15 will have deeper voices. Whiskers also appear on the face towards the end of the process. During puberty, muscle strength increases as a result of testosterone.

Self-esteem and puberty amongst boys

Whilst early puberty in girls has significant negative outcomes in terms of body image, the same is not true for boys. In boys, early puberty is often associated with positive body image, but this might not be the full picture as according to Bee (2005), there may be longer-term negative effects, such as increased aggression and vulnerability when coping with stressful life events.

Having said this, late development in boys seems to have more problems. Many of the characteristics associated with masculinity, such as strength, power and even pitch of voice, are the results of testosterone production. Thus a boy who has not yet gone through puberty is likely to have anxieties about his 'maleness' and may not feel positive about himself as a result.

What does it mean in practice?

Supporting young people during puberty

- Help young people understand the process of puberty.

- Acknowledge their fears about their size and shape.

- Be aware that a young person may be teased during this time. Make sure there is a strong anti-bullying policy in your setting.

- Look out for areas where young people may excel and gain confidence.

Sexual relationships and the law

In theory, sexual intercourse below the age of 16 is illegal in the UK. In reality, the interpretation of this law depends on the ages of both partners. Young people of the same age or very similar ages who have consensual sex do not usually have any action taken against them. The situation changes radically if an adult has sex with a young person below the age of 16. This is because the relationship is usually seen as exploitative and the young person therefore needs to be protected. This same principle applies where there are discrepancies between the ages of young people, even if both are under 16 years old. Thus, a boy of 15 may very well be prosecuted for having sex with a 12-year-old girl.

Whilst the law forbids sexual intercourse before the age of 16, sexual advice, contraception and even abortions can be provided for young people below the legal age of consent without parental permission. This has led to some well-publicised cases of parents finding out that an abortion has taken place without their knowledge.

▲ Developing sexual relationships is an important part of maturing, but there are laws in place to protect young people

Effects of early sexual activity

Early sexual activity can have a negative effect on young people for a variety of reasons. Firstly, there are the high rates of teenage pregnancies and abortions. Outcomes for children born to teenage parents are generally less favourable than those born to parents in their twenties and beyond. This is likely to link to economic difficulties as well as maturity levels, since raising children is hugely demanding, especially if no support is available.

As well as the risk of pregnancy, young people also run the dangers of picking up a sexually transmitted disease (STD). The prevalence of STDs in young people is currently on the increase. Chlamydia, in particular, is giving health professionals cause for concern, as it is currently the most common STD. It is seen as a 'ticking time bomb', as it is a disease relatively free of symptoms but which can leave women infertile if untreated. Chlamydia rates amongst the under-20s are particularly high. Estimates vary but it is suggested that at least 1 in 10 women are affected by it, although, because of its lack of symptoms, the true rates might be much higher.

Factors affecting early sexual activity are:

- **Relationships with parents** Young people who have good relationships with their parents, and where discussion about sex has been available, seem to fare better. They are more likely to delay sexual activity.

- **Sex education** Good sex education in schools is often seen as vital, but many young people report that it is not sufficient or useful. Sex education in other countries, which have lower rates of pregnancy, is often of a better quality. The most effective sex education seems to combine the 'mechanics' of sex and contraception with giving young people negotiation skills, together with exploration of the emotional side of relationships.

- **Socio-economic** Conception and pregnancy rates seem to be higher in areas of social deprivation. The reason given is that becoming a parent may seem more fulfilling and desirable than unemployment or working in a low-paid, low-status job.

- **Separation and divorce** There is some evidence that suggests that girls are more likely to be sexually active earlier if they are in lone-parent households.

- **Age of mother** Statistically, teenage mothers are more likely to have daughters who become teenage mothers. This again might be linked to the social and economic disadvantage that having a child early brings.

- **Peer group** Early sexual activity can vary enormously between groups of young people. Thus a young person who is in a group where sexual activity is not yet the 'norm' may delay their activity.

- **Alcohol** Alcohol also seems to play a part in unplanned and unprotected sexual activity (see article on page 164).

THE SCOTSMAN 24 March 2005

The sex lives of Scotland's children

By Claire Smith

More than a quarter of 14-year-old Scottish girls have had sex and almost half of them regret it, according to a new survey.

A nationwide poll by girls' magazine *Bliss* discovered 26 per cent of 14-year-olds in Scotland had had sex, compared with 22 per cent nationwide. Of the teenage girls surveyed, 60 per cent said they were drunk the first time they had sex, a quarter said they were "forced into it" and 6 per cent said they were assaulted.

The UK has the highest rates of teenage pregnancy in Europe and the incidence of sexually transmitted diseases among the young is also on the increase. Two-thirds of sexually active 14-year-olds surveyed admitted they had had unprotected sex and half had taken the morning-after pill or had a pregnancy test. Those having sex had an average of three partners and almost half had had a one-night stand.

Seventy per cent said they wished they had more information about love and sex to help them make the right choices in life. And 49 per cent said they have had a sexual experience they regret, with 29 per cent saying they "didn't even like" their sexual partner.

Alice McLeod, from Glasgow University Urban Studies department, who has carried out studies on teenage pregnancy in Scotland, said the results showed girls were having sex when they were not ready. "Improved sex education isn't just about knowing what contraceptives to use but knowing you cannot have sex and you can wait until a later date. But there will always be a certain group of teenagers who will want to have sex at an early age and these need proper access to education and contraception."

The editor of *Bliss*, Lisa Smosarski, said the results were shocking and showed that teenage girls needed sex and health education with more emphasis on relationships and self-confidence.

Issues – Is abstinence the way forward?

Whilst the fact that the UK has a high rate of teenage pregnancy is not contested, approaches on how to deal with it vary considerably. There are many health professionals who believe that sex education is the best approach, whilst others blame sex education, suggesting that it encourages early sexual intimacy! Recently imported from the US is an initiative known as the 'Silver Ring Thing'. The idea is to encourage teenagers to sign up to not having sex until after marriage and to show their commitment by wearing a silver ring. Advocates of this approach believe that abstinence takes pressure off young people and claim that, at the very least, it delays the start of sexual relationships. Critics suggest that the initiative is simply a cunning way of indoctrinating young people into a religious faith. They point to some research that suggests that 88 per cent of those on the American programme broke their vows and were then less likely to use any contraception.

Interview – *John, 18 years old*

Q. Why do you wear a silver ring?

A. I wear a silver ring because I am a Christian. I heard about the Silver Ring Thing and thought it was a good idea. It takes a lot of pressure off of you as everyone immediately knows where you stand.

Q. How do people react?

A. I have found that there is a lot of interest. Once I explain why I am wearing it the reactions are quite positive. I suppose that I am quite honest about it.

▲ The wearing of a silver ring demonstrates the pledge not to have sex until after marriage

What does it mean in practice?

Helping young people to make decisions on sexual activity

Supporting young people in this area is complex. However, good body image and confidence as well as knowledge seem to be fundamental. Young people need to have good information about sex and contraception, also about relationships and how to negotiate and communicate with partners. Parents too may need to be provided with suggestions and support, so that they can feel confident to talk to their children. Some ways to help include providing:

■ signposting information, e.g. leaflets

■ information about local support from health professionals, such as health promotion teams

■ relaxed environments where young people can enjoy being together without pressure.

Nutrition

Food and drink play a major role in the healthy growth and development of children of all ages. Good nutrition seems to have positive effects in terms of overall health, but also on growth, concentration and behaviour. It has become a 'hot topic' and has received plenty of publicity, mainly as a result of increased rates of obesity in children.

What constitutes good nutrition?

Food is broken down by the body into chemicals that provide energy and nutrients. Good nutrition for children is about getting the right balance of food for their age and activity level. As children get older their requirements for energy and nutrients change, so it is useful to have some knowledge of these changes and also about the different nutrients.

Nutrients are the components of foods that assist the body in some way. Most foods contain at least one nutrient. They are generally put into five different groups as shown in Table 5.2.

Table 5.2 **Nutrient groups**

Nutrient	Key functions	Sources of nutrient
Carbohydrate	Provides energy	Bread, rice, potatoes, sweet potatoes, yams, bananas
Fat	Provides energy and helps absorption of vitamins A and E	Olive oil, meat, dairy products such as butter, milk, yoghurt
Protein	Aids growth and is required for general repair and maintenance of the body	Meat, eggs, dairy products, lentils, peas, beans, nuts
Vitamins	Required in relatively small quantities, but each has a particular role in the body, e.g. vitamin C is needed for healthy skin	Vitamin A – found in dairy products; requires fat in order to be absorbed Vitamin B – found in many carbohydrate-rich foods Vitamin C – found in most fresh fruit and vegetables; absorbed more efficiently when a source of iron is present, e.g. green leaf vegetables, meat or egg Vitamin D – found naturally in sunlight, but also in fortified foods such as margarine Vitamin E – found in dairy produce; requires fat in order to be absorbed
Minerals	There are numerous minerals required for healthy growth and maintenance of the body. Levels of calcium need to be sufficient for children of all ages. Also, iron for teenage girls	Calcium – found in dairy produce such as cheese and eggs Iron – found in meat, green leaf vegetables such as spinach, eggs

Note: whilst water is essential for the functioning of the body, it is not actually considered to be a nutrient.

The body also needs sufficient energy to function. Energy is usually measured in kilojoules or kilocalories, although most people talk about 'calories'. The amount of energy that is put into the body needs to match its requirements, otherwise the body stores any surplus as fatty deposits. Energy is found in differing quantities in two key nutrients: fat and carbohydrate. Fat contains significant quantities of calories and so intake needs to be monitored, although it should never be eliminated without professional advice as some intake of fat is essential for health.

The story so far...

Early nutritional needs

In the first few months, babies grow and develop rapidly. They should ideally be breast fed until 6 months old when weaning should take place. Weaning allows babies to take in more energy, but particularly iron, which is not available in milk.

From the ages of 1–3, toddlers require energy-dense diets. Their stomachs are small, but relative to their size their energy levels are high. This is why full fat milk is recommended for at least the first two years and high fibre diets are not suitable.

From 4–6 years, energy requirements continue to increase, but children need higher levels of protein. Babies and children are also learning attitudes towards food, as well as developing tastes for foods.

Nutritional needs 7–10 years

During this period, children begin to need more protein and energy. They also need increased amounts of other minerals and vitamins, except for vitamins A, B1 (thiamine) and C. Differences in energy requirements between boys and girls in this period are relatively slight.

Nutritional needs 11–14 years

From the age of 11 onwards, nutritional and energy requirements for boys and girls begin to differ more markedly.

- **Boys** Overall they will need increased amounts of all the vitamins and minerals, but particularly calcium where the levels need to double. They will also need significantly more energy and about 50 per cent more protein.

■ **Girls** Girls also need approximately 50 per cent more protein and have higher energy requirements, but less than boys. They will need more iron once their periods begin, as well as increases in other vitamins, with the exception of three of the vitamin B group: thiamine, niacin and pyridoxine (vitamin B6). Their iron requirement almost doubles once periods begin and this higher level is needed until menopause. Calcium intake should also increase sharply.

> **Did you know?**
>
> Higher intakes of iron are required for girls once they start their periods. Low intakes can cause anaemia for which symptoms include tiredness and fainting.

Nutritional needs 15–18 years

Energy demand and the differences between the sexes both continue to increase during this period.

■ **Boys** They continue to require high levels of energy, protein and vitamins. They also continue to need calcium for skeletal development.

■ **Girls** They also continue to need increased levels of energy, protein and vitamins. A key difference from boys is their continued requirement for high levels of iron.

Table 5.3 Energy requirements for children and young people 7–18 years given in kcal

Age	Boys	Girls
7–10	1,970	1,740
11–14	2,220	1,845
15–18	2,755	2,110

Source: British Nutrition Foundation, 2004

Development and nutritional needs

There are significant consequences for children and young people if their nutritional needs are not met, as Figure 5.1 shows. The term used where a diet is lacking in nutrients is 'malnourished'. Ironically in the UK, a country that is relatively wealthy, there are many children who are malnourished, yet who are eating either too much in terms of quantity or, more often, the wrong balance of foods.

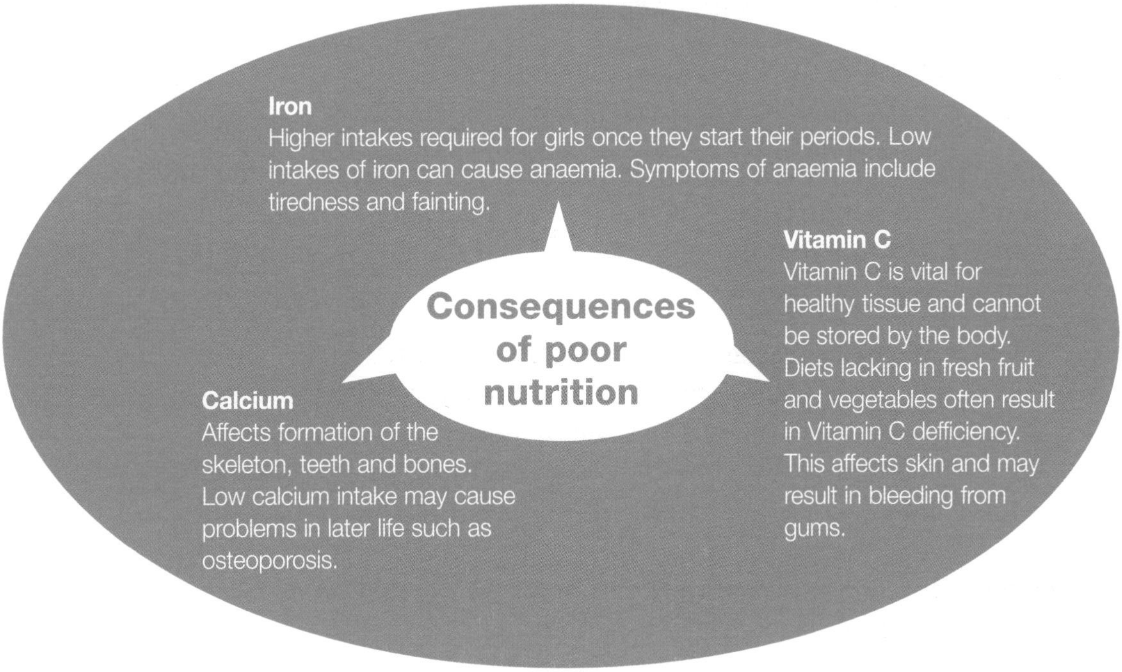

Iron
Higher intakes required for girls once they start their periods. Low intakes of iron can cause anaemia. Symptoms of anaemia include tiredness and fainting.

Consequences of poor nutrition

Vitamin C
Vitamin C is vital for healthy tissue and cannot be stored by the body. Diets lacking in fresh fruit and vegetables often result in Vitamin C defficiency. This affects skin and may result in bleeding from gums.

Calcium
Affects formation of the skeleton, teeth and bones. Low calcium intake may cause problems in later life such as osteoporosis.

▲ Figure 5.1

What does it mean in practice?

Helping to ensure that children and young people have a healthy diet

▓ Be aware of children and young people who may be skipping meals.

▓ Help children and young people eat well by providing freshly prepared foods wherever possible.

▓ Expect that teenagers will need snacks, but avoid providing foods that are high in calories yet low in nutrients, e.g. fizzy drinks.

▓ Look for ways of encouraging children and young people to eat five portions of fruit and vegetables a day.

▓ Make sure that teenage girls' diets are sufficiently high in iron and calcium.

▓ Provide diets that have sufficient protein and also calcium for teenage boys.

▓ Act as a good role model by, for example, drinking plenty of water.

▓ Keep up to date with nutritional advice by using the Food Standards Agency website. A link to this website has been made available at www.heinemann.co.uk/hotlinks. Simply enter the express code 983XP.

Overweight and obese children

Childhood weight gain and the overall quality of children's diets are currently 'hot topics'. There has been a relatively sudden increase in the numbers of children and young people who are either overweight or obese. Table 5.4 clearly shows this trend, though note that it only includes numbers of those who are obese, not overweight.

Table 5.4 **Trends in obesity rates 1995–2004**

	Boys		Girls	
Age	1995	2004	1995	2004
2–10	10%	16%	12%	12%
11–15	14%	24%	15%	26%

(Source: Health Survey for England 2004, Department of Health)

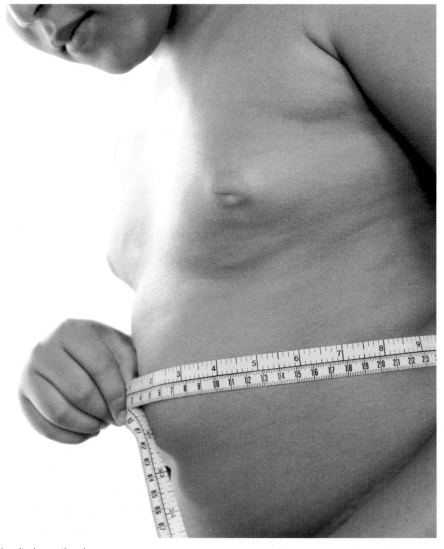

Childhood obesity is on the rise

What does it mean in practice?

Helping children and young people who are overweight or obese

This is a complex issue, as both physical and emotional factors tend to be at work. Children and young people who become overweight are likely to develop poor body image, which in turn can encourage them to use food for comfort. They may also find it harder and less rewarding to take exercise, especially participation in competitive games or when others start to comment about their size. As physical activity is essential to avoid a surplus of calories, and also important for maintaining health, this can lead to further weight gain and even health problems.

Information about food and nutrition is also important, especially for teenagers, who increasingly have more control over what and when they eat. Providing information, and also equipping young people with the skills they need to prepare food, can therefore be helpful.

- Be a good role model – enjoy your own food, but make sure that you are eating a balanced diet.

- Encourage children and young people to prepare their own food.

- Provide healthy snacks and drinks.

- Avoid using food for rewards and treats.

- Organise events such as tasting days, recipe swapping or cooking classes/competitions.

- Help children to come to settings using 'walking buses' (see the section on physical activity on page 173 for more information).

- Look for ways of helping physical activity to be fun and participative, e.g. water slides, balloon football.

- Provide information about activities, interests and walks in your local area.

- Make contacts with local health professionals, e.g. dieticians, health promotion unit.

- Think about ways in which you can help children and young people gain a positive body image.

Eating disorders

There is a range of eating disorders that can affect children and young people. The most common are shown in Table 5.5. Reasons for eating disorders are complex and there is some speculation that some young people may even be genetically pre-disposed. However, at the heart of most eating disorders is some level of anxiety and depression. Many begin with a simple wish to be slimmer and dissatisfaction with body shape and size.

Whilst eating disorders can begin at any age, even in adulthood, the majority occur between 15–25 years of age, although children as young as 7 and 8 have been affected. In general terms, girls are more likely to be affected by eating disorders than boys. This might be a result of society's interest in beauty and slimness and the way in which girls' physical appearance is often commented on during their childhood.

Table 5.5 **Common eating disorders**

Disorder	Physical signs	Behavioural signs	Psychological signs
Anorexia nervosa	Severe weight loss Periods stopping (amenorrhoea) Hormonal changes in men and boys Difficulty sleeping Dizziness Stomach pains Constipation Poor circulation and feeling cold	Wanting to be left alone Wearing baggy clothes Excessive exercising Lying about eating Denying there is a problem Difficulty concentrating Wanting to have control	Intense fear of gaining weight Depression Feeling emotional Obsession with dieting Mood swings Distorted perception of body weight and size
Bulimia nervosa	Sore throat or swollen glands Stomach pains Mouth infections Irregular periods Dry or poor skin Difficulty sleeping Sensitive or damaged teeth	Eating large quantities of food Being sick after eating Being secretive	Feeling ashamed, depressed and guilty Feeling out of control Mood swings
Binge eating	Weight gain	Eating large quantities of food Eating inappropriate food Being secretive	Feeling depressed and out of control Mood swings Emotional behaviour

Source: Eating Disorders Association

What does it mean in practice?

Supporting children and young people who may have eating disorders

It is important to be aware that some children, and especially young people, may be developing eating disorders.

■ Look out for behavioural signs.

■ Be supportive, friendly and non-judgemental.

■ Avoid focusing only on food.

■ Look for ways of helping young people feel good about themselves.

■ Provide information, e.g. websites, so that they can learn more about what is happening.

Physical activity

Physical activity plays a significant part in children's and young people's health, growth and development (see Figure 5.2). Current advice on physical activity is that all children and young people should have at least one hour's exercise a day of moderate intensity. Moderate intensity includes some vigorous activity such as running or doing something else that increases the heart rate. Some vigorous activity is thought to assist the body's cardiovascular system and help prevent some diseases in later life.

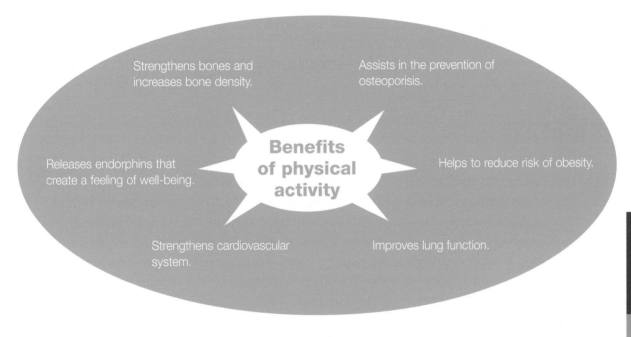

Strengthens bones and increases bone density.

Assists in the prevention of osteoporisis.

Releases endorphins that create a feeling of well-being.

Benefits of physical activity

Helps to reduce risk of obesity.

Strengthens cardiovascular system.

Improves lung function.

▲ **Figure 5.2** The benefits of physical activity

Trends in activity rates

Overall there has been a decline in the amount of physical activity and exercise that children and young people are getting. In 2005, researchers in Bristol looked at activity rates for 11-year-olds and concluded that 90 per cent of them were not meeting the recommended activity levels.

Primary school children

Some schools do not have the playing fields and space available for children to engage in physical activity. Playground games were on the decline, but many schools now teach skipping and other games so more children can become active at playtime. In addition, many schools had reduced the amount of PE time as part of changes to the curriculum, although the government has since issued new guidelines.

The numbers of children who walk to school has also been an issue, with many parents dropping their children off in cars. This is partly to do with parental fears over road safety, as well as other concerns over personal safety. In some areas of the UK, schemes to encourage children to walk to school have proved popular. The schemes, often called 'walking buses', create supervised routes for children to walk to school in local neighbourhoods.

In addition, physical activity for children out of school hours has also decreased. This has been blamed on fear by parents of letting their children play outside unsupervised, and also the poor provision of play areas. These factors are probably exacerbated by the advent of a wider choice of media entertainment, such as computers, computer games consoles and television.

> **Did you know?**
>
> The proportion of children aged 5–10 who walked to school fell from 61 per cent in 1992–94 to 52 per cent in 2002–03.

Young people aged 11–16 years

There is a dramatic downward shift in the number of young people who engage in physical activity, but strikingly amongst girls, although this is replicated in boys later on. The suggested reasons for this can be found below but, for both sexes, current trends are a matter of deep concern, as physical activity has health benefits in later life. Bone density, for example, is built up through weight-bearing exercise and intake of sufficient calcium. The teenage years are vital for both of these. Reduced activity also sets a trend for later life, so those teenagers who are active are more likely to continue their level of physical activity as adults.

Differences between boys and girls

Boys and girls seem to show different levels of physical activity from about the age of 2 years. Whilst at first the differences are slight, they become more pronounced in adolescence with just 41 per cent of girls aged 13–15 meeting the recommended levels of physical activity, compared with 68 per cent of boys.

Reasons why adolescent girls' activity rates decline

It is not totally clear why girls' activity rates decline, but the following reasons have been suggested:

- **Body image** During adolescence, girls' body shapes change and some girls become very self-conscious. Girls may also associate sweating and muscle development with being unfeminine. Sport is also perceived as a 'boy' activity and so may not be valued.

- **Influence of the media** Whilst there are many male sporting role models, there are fewer such women in the public eye. Teenage magazines tend to emphasise fashion, make-up and looking good, rather than fitness and sports.

- **Dislike of competitive activities** Whilst many boys enjoy some elements of competitive activities, the same is not true for many girls from 11 years onwards. Activities that seem to have social elements to them are often more popular.

What does it mean in practice?

Ways to encourage physical activity

- Act as a good role model – show children and young people that you enjoy physical activity.

- Provide plenty of opportunities for outdoor play and games.

- Make sure that physical activity is seen as enjoyable and fun.

- Consider the issues of competition, especially in relation to older girls.

- Avoid being only 'sport' focused – other enjoyable activities, such as ice skating, salsa dancing, bowling, skateboarding and cycling, are beneficial too.

- Be sensitive and aware of issues such as changing body shape and the onset of periods for teenage girls.

- Organise fun events that involve the whole family, e.g. walks and picnics.

- Look out for national and local grants available to improve facilities and provide equipment.

Smoking

Whilst overall numbers of young people smoking have been quite stable over the last few years, it still remains a significant health issue. Young people who smoke are more likely to develop respiratory problems and also more likely to become addicted to nicotine. This is perhaps illustrated by the statistic that 70 per cent of adult smokers began smoking between the ages of 11 and 15.

Influences

So why do young people continue to smoke, given that there is now plenty of information that smoking is dangerous for health and anti-smoking campaigns begin in primary schools? As with many other areas of development, the answers are quite complex and there are many factors at work.

▲ Some young people may smoke because they see a celebrity they admire smoking

Adult role models

Adults smoking, even around young children, seem to have some effect on whether or not young people will go on to smoke. A child growing up with both parents smoking is three times more likely to become a smoker. Whilst this may not seem unremarkable, what is surprising is that ASH (the anti-smoking campaign group) suggests that, already by the age of 5, most children know what a cigarette is for and how to hold it, even if their parents are non-smokers. This links back to social cognitive learning theory (see page 128).

In addition to adult members of children's and young people's families, other role models also seem significant. Film stars, celebrities and models who are photographed or appear in films smoking are seen as creating the perception in young people that smoking gives higher social status.

Advertising

Advertising also seems to affect young people. Before the ban on cigarette advertising took place, young people consistently smoked those brands that were the most heavily advertised, thus showing that advertising can make a difference.

Peer pressure

Young people report that they are influenced by older siblings who smoke, and also their friends. This is not dissimilar to the findings about drug taking, as here too young people are more likely to be introduced to drugs via friends or older siblings.

Psychological factors

Some young people also seem more vulnerable than others to starting smoking. They tend to be those who have become disenchanted at school and may be less academic. There also seems to be some link between relationships with family members, especially parents. Where young people feel that they do not 'belong' to a family or are not supported, they are more likely to smoke. A sense of belonging, both in school and family situations, seems therefore to be a protective factor.

Differences between the genders

For many years, more boys than girls smoked. Today, we have a reverse of this pattern and since 1993 girls are significantly more likely to smoke than boys. In 2005, 25 per cent of girls aged 15 were smoking compared with 16 per cent of boys. One suggested reason for this difference is that many teenage girls believe that smoking will relieve symptoms of anxiety and depression, so use it as a source of self-medication. Another reason links back to adult role models. Boys are more likely to choose 'sporting' role models, such as footballers, who usually do not smoke.

Age and smoking

Smoking is not usually an issue until young people reach secondary education, as few smoke before the age of 11. From 11 onwards there is a gradual increase in the numbers that smoke so that, whilst only 1 per cent of 11-year-olds regularly smoke, 20 per cent of 15-year-olds smoke.

You may find it interesting to ask a cross-section of young people:

■ At what age did you begin to smoke?

■ Where did you get your cigarettes from?

■ Why do you think you started smoking?

What does it mean in practice?

Helping children and young people to avoid smoking

- Adults are hugely influential – do not smoke around children of any age.

- With young people, make sure that evidence of smoking is not available, e.g. ashtrays in staff rooms or adults with a cigarette packet in their pocket.

- Encourage children and young people to enjoy sport.

- Look for ways of engaging with those who smoke, e.g. helping to organise activities, listening to them.

- Look out for signs of anxiety and depression.

- Provide good health promotion information.

- Have a clear policy on smoking.

▲ A significant minority of young people have used drugs such as cannabis

Drug and alcohol use

Each year, the Department of Health commissions a survey to look at smoking, drinking and drug use amongst young people. The 2005 survey shows that cannabis is the most commonly used drug amongst young people, with glue and other substance sniffing far less used. As with smoking and drinking alcohol, there is increased use as young people get older. Thus, whilst 6 per cent of 11-year-olds are taking drugs, this figure rises to around 34 per cent at 15 years of age.

The effects of cannabis

Cannabis provides a sedative effect that can give young people a pleasant feeling of relaxation, hence the terms 'chilled' or 'spaced out'. It does not have the same effects on everyone. It may make some feel sick, or even panicky and anxious.

DRUGSCOPE 3 June 2004

People in the UK amongst biggest users of cannabis

A report released today shows rates of cannabis use amongst young people in the UK are some of the highest in the world. 'Young people's health in context' published by the World Health Organisation (WHO) Regional Office for Europe shows that, on average, 22 per cent of 15-year-olds across the WHO European Region and North America have tried cannabis and 8 per cent report using it regularly.

Rates of use in England, Scotland and Wales were considerably higher than this however, at 40.5 per cent, 37.4 per cent and 34 per cent respectively for 'ever used', and 34.9 per cent, 30.4 per cent and 25.3 per cent respectively for 'used in last 12 months'.

Harry Shapiro of DrugScope commented: "The results of this latest survey are not particularly surprising. In recent years successive reports have repeatedly shown young people in the UK to be some of the biggest consumers of illegal drugs in the world. It therefore follows that cannabis use, as the most widely available drug, will be high."

He continued: "However, although this is concerning, we must also put it in perspective. The latest figures from the Department of Health showed that 21 per cent of 11- to 15-year-olds had taken drugs in the last year. This means that the vast majority of school-aged children never use drugs."

'Young people's health in context' reports on the most recent survey of the Health Behaviour in School-aged Children study, which covered almost 162,000 young people aged 11, 13 and 15 years in 35 countries and regions in the WHO European Region and North America.

Concerns

Whilst the UK government recently downgraded cannabis from a Class B drug to a Class C drug, health professionals remain clear that it is not a totally harmless drug, especially for young people. This is not always the perception held by young people themselves, who may feel that it is totally risk-free. The effects of cannabis are linked to the amount used and also the type and strength used. Cannabis also seems to affect some people more than others.

■ **Gateway drug?** Many adults worry that cannabis acts as a gateway drug so that, from this drug, young people are likely to go on to experiment with other more dangerous substances. However, the statistics do not bear this out, although some young people will later on try out other drugs. Use of cannabis can, however, create contacts between young people and drug dealers and these relationships might mean that other drugs are 'pushed'.

■ **Addiction?** Whilst for most young people cannabis is not addictive, young people can get used to taking it and so become dependent. This means that, whilst they may not be physically addicted to it, they may be using it as an emotional and social support.

■ **Effects on learning?** There is some research that clearly shows that concentration and learning are harmed by regular cannabis use. Whether these effects are temporary or create permanent difficulties is a source of debate and research. Regular use can create feelings of lethargy and tiredness, so young people may fail to turn up to activities or lessons. Overall school performance tends to drop, but it is hard to know whether cannabis use is the cause or if a young person was already becoming disengaged from schooling. The Department of Health's report on the 2005 survey does show that 57 per cent of those truanting or excluded from school will use drugs.

▲ Drug use can seriously affect mental health and well-b

■ **Mental health?** A worrying aspect of cannabis use is the probable link with mental health. Young people smoking cannabis before the age of 15 seem to be far more vulnerable to mental health problems than those who either smoke later as an adult or not at all. Particularly at risk are those young people who may have a genetic predisposition to schizophrenia, so health professionals strongly advise them not to take cannabis. The reasons why young people seem to be more vulnerable may lie within the brain. It is thought that the chemicals within cannabis and particularly 'skunk', the stronger version, interfere with normal brain development.

Did you know?

In 2005, 19 per cent of secondary school aged children had taken drugs in the last year

Helping young people

Drug awareness education seems to be the most effective way of helping young people. The 'all drugs are bad' message tends not to be effective, as some young people will look around at their friends or older siblings and see for themselves that they appear healthy and not addicted. This means that, today, the focus is about providing young people with accurate information, and also the skills and confidence to decline drugs without being alienated from their peers or friends. This is important, as most young people will be offered drugs when they are in social situations. The popular image of drug dealers stalking the gates of schools and other establishments is not accurate. Drugs are more often offered by older siblings, friends or relatives.

Signs that a young person may be using drugs

Spotting that a young person is using drugs may not always be easy, but behavioural changes may often be an indication. These might include:

- tiredness and lethargy
- moodiness
- lack of money or stealing
- poor school performance
- withdrawal from previous friendships and family
- lack of interest in hobbies and leisure activities previously enjoyed
- changed eating patterns
- possession of cigarette papers, lighters, small pieces of clingfilm, transfers, pipes, etc.

What does it mean in practice?

Ways of helping young people avoid drugs

- Have a clear policy on drugs and drug awareness.
- Invite local drug advisors in to talk to young people.
- Provide sources of accurate information. A link to the 'talktofrank' website has been made available at www.heinemann.co.uk/hotlinks. Enter the express code 983XP.
- Find out more information yourself about current drugs and trends in use.
- Take a non-judgemental listening approach to young people and drug issues.
- Provide parents with information about drugs and drug use.

Issues – Drug testing

The use of drug testing in secondary schools is currently being considered. Whilst some advocate its use, others such as the charity DrugScope are very concerned and believe that this will create tension and affect relationships between pupils and teachers.

DAILY MAIL MAY 30 2006

Pupils to face random drug tests at school

Random drug testing could be introduced in all secondary schools to help children resist peer pressure and "just say no" to drugs. The first UK school to introduce random drug testing posted their best ever exam results following a year-long pilot last year. Now the Government has signalled it is keen for random drug testing to be rolled out nationwide, depending on the success of a pilot scheme they plan to introduce in Kent schools in autumn. Headteachers and parents will be asked if they would like their pupils to take part in the pilot.

Kent was chosen by the Department for Education and Skills for the pilot because it was a local headteacher who first introduced it in his school with astonishing results. Peter Walker is the former head-teacher of The Abbey School in Faversham, Kent. It is a non-selective specialist school for business and enterprise whose catchment area includes the second most deprived council ward in the county.

Last year 600 random drug tests were carried out on pupils aged between 11 and 18. Testing was done by mouth swabs for all classes of drugs, including cannabis, cocaine and heroin. Of the school's 960 pupils, 86 per cent consented to be randomly tested. Only one child tested positive, for cannabis.

Mr Walker said: "We had our best set of exam results in the school's history. There's less disruption in the classroom, fewer incidents in the playground or on the way to school. Children feel that they are far better protected. The biggest reason for taking drugs is peer group pressure. It looks like we may well have found a way for children to have a viable way of saying no to their peer group."

Alcohol use

Whilst drug use tends to gain quite a lot of attention, some young people are also using alcohol. The Department of Health 2005 survey showed that, in the 11–15 age range, 22 per cent of pupils had drunk alcohol in the last week. As with drug use, the percentage of young people who drink increases with their age. Whilst alcohol consumption is relatively low amongst 11- and 12-year-olds, it is much higher amongst 15-year-olds with 45 per cent of this age drinking regularly.

The survey also shows that drinking is often done at weekends, with boys favouring beer and cider and girls preferring 'alco-pops'. Relatively high levels of alcohol are also drunk, with girls now drinking similar amounts to boys.

▲ Nearly half of all 15-year-olds drink alcohol regularly

Effects of alcohol

The short-term effects of drinking are behavioural, with teenage boys more likely to be involved in fights. For girls, alcohol may affect their judgement about sexual activity, as the article 'The sex lives of Scotland's children' on page 164 indicates. Experts are also concerned about the longer-term impact of drinking relatively heavily at an early age. They predict that the culture of drinking heavily in short bursts, known as 'binge drinking', will result in more cases of liver diseases in the future.

What does it mean in practice?

Tackling alcohol abuse

■ Have a clear policy on alcohol use in your setting.

■ Provide young people with information about alcohol.

■ If you drink alcohol, act as a good role model.

■ Provide activities that are enjoyable for young people.

Show your knowledge

1 How might expectations of children vary according to their height?

2 How does stamina in young people compare to children under 5 years old?

3 Name the five nutrient groups and give examples of possible food sources.

4 Identify the key hormones that are involved in puberty of girls and boys.

5 What are the possible effects of early puberty in girls?

6 Give an example of an eating disorder and list two associated signs of it.

7 Name two influences that may result in young people smoking.

8 What are the potential effects of cannabis use in young people?

9 Why is it essential that young people are given accurate information in relation to drugs?

10 List three reasons why girls aged 11–16 may not participate in physical activities.

Further sources of information

Links to websites providing sources of information on the following have been provided at www.heinemann.co.uk/hotlinks. Simply enter the express code 983XP to access the links.

■ Statistics from the National Health Service

■ Anti-tobacco campaigning groups

■ Health topics relating to 11- to 14-year-olds

■ Health topics relating to 14- to 16-year-olds.

Index

and personality 33–4
and sex-role stereotypes 51
social cognitive learning 128–31
legislation 4–7, 161–2
life stages, Erikson's 41–3

M

mathematics
and abstract reasoning 147
attitude towards 148
and information processing 148
support in learning 149
media
and decline in reading 138
effects of violence 131
influence on self-esteem 53
sporting role models 54, 175
memory 118–19
metacognition 120
metamemory 121
retrieval 120
strategies 119–20
mental health
and cannabis use 180
useful contacts 28
metacognition 120
metamemory 121
modelling
learning through 128
and personality 35
as teaching strategy 130
moral development 91
behaviourist theories 93
Kohlberg's stages of 96–7
operant conditioning 93
Piaget's stages of 95
psychoanalytic theories 92–3
social cognitive theory 94
and social environment 98
young children 92
MORI crime surveys 23, 24
motor movement development
157–8
movement, development of 157–8
multiple intelligences 136–7
muscle and fat, development of
156–7
myelinisation 106, 107–8

N

naive realism 113
National Curriculum 16, 17
in England 139–41
nature versus nurture debate
and intelligence 133
and personality 31–3
and spatial skills of boys 134
'needs-orientated reasoning'
99–100
negative reinforcers 123–4
neglect 8, 9–10
neglected children 79
neurons 104–5
neuroticism 30
'no blame' approach to bullying 89

Northern Ireland, education in 17
numeracy
early development of 147
strategies for learning 148
nutrition 166
children's needs 167–8
eating disorders 171–2
effects of poor 168–9
and obesity 170–1

O

obesity in children 170–1
Oedipus complex 40, 52
omega-3 108
onlooker intervention 101
openness/intellect, personality
trait 30
operant conditioning
applications of 127
cognitive development 123–7
and moral development 93
ossification 158
overweight children 170–1

P

parents
attitudes towards gender roles 51
conflict with teenagers 67–8
divorce and separation 69
influencing personality 33–4,
36–7, 41, 53
working with 68
see also attachment
partial reinforcement 34
peer comparison 54
peer pressure 83
and drugs 182
effect on boys' attainment 138
and smoking 177
persona dolls 81
personality
and attachment 62
behaviourist approaches 34–5
Big Five traits 30
and birth order 35–6
and gender 36–7
and learning 43
learning theory 33–4
nature versus nurture 31–3
psychoanalytic theories 37–43,
52
social cognitive theory 35
'pester power' 26
phonics, reading method 138, 143
physical abuse 8, 10
physical activity
benefits of 173
decline in 173–4
gender differences 174–5
ways to encourage 175
physical appearance
and adult expectations 154
and eating disorders 171
and popularity 80
and self-esteem 56

physical development 152
and alcohol use 183–4
and drug use 178–82
effect of poverty on 19–20
fat and muscles 156–7
growth 152–4
motor movement 157–8
nutrition 166–72
physical activity 173–5
puberty 158–65
and smoking 175–8
and stamina 154–6
Piaget, Jean
cognitive development 109–13,
147
stages of moral development 95
pituitary gland 153, 159
play
gender differences 77
gender segregation 76
interests and friendships 74–5
popularity 78–80
positive reinforcers 123–4
post-conventional morality 97
poverty
effects on children 19–21
initiatives to eradicate 21–2
and IQ test results 133
practical intelligence 136
pre-conventional morality 96
primary reinforcers 125
principled morality 97
pro-social development 99–100
behaviourist approach 100
and bullying 101–2
encouraging 100
protection of children 8–14
psychoanalytical theories
and gender concept 52
moral development 92–3
of personality
Erikson's 41–3
Freud's 37–41, 52
psychological factors influencing
smoking 177
psychosexual stages, Freudian
theory 39–40
puberty 158–9
in boys 160–1
in girls 159–60
and self-concept 157
and sexual relationships 161–2

R

reading
approaches to learning 142–3
decline in time spent 138, 143
and dyslexia 144–6
early development 142
functional readers 143
methods of teaching 138
reinforcement 34, 35, 123
applying 127
effectiveness of positive 124
intrinsic 129–30
primary and secondary 125